Miniature Crocheting and Knitting for Dollhouses

Rosemary Drysdale

Dover Publications, Inc., New York

Published in Canada by General Publishing Company, Ltd., 30 Lesmill Road, Don Mills, Toronto, Ontario.
Published in the United Kingdom by Constable and Company, Ltd..

Miniature Crocheting and Knitting for Dollhouses is a new work, first published by Dover Publications Inc., in 1981.

Edited by Linda Macho
Book design by Paula Goldstein

International Standard Book Number: 0-486-23964-0
Library of Congress Catalog Card Number: 81-67528

Manufactured in the United States of America
Dover Publications, Inc.
180 Varick Street
New York, N.Y. 10014

Contents

Metric Conversion Chart

CONVERTING INCHES TO CENTIMETERS AND YARDS TO METERS

mm — millimeters   cm — centimeters   m — meters

INCHES INTO MILLIMETERS AND CENTIMETERS
(Slightly rounded off for convenience)

inches	mm		cm	inches	cm	inches	cm	inches	cm
⅛	3mm			5	12.5	21	53.5	38	96.5
¼	6mm			5½	14	22	56	39	99
⅜	10mm	or	1cm	6	15	23	58.5	40	101.5
½	13mm	or	1.3cm	7	18	24	61	41	104
⅝	15mm	or	1.5cm	8	20.5	25	63.5	42	106.5
¾	20mm	or	2cm	9	23	26	66	43	109
⅞	22mm	or	2.2cm	10	25.5	27	68.5	44	112
1	25mm	or	2.5cm	11	28	28	71	45	114.5
1¼	32mm	or	3.2cm	12	30.5	29	73.5	46	117
1½	38mm	or	3.8cm	13	33	30	76	47	119.5
1¾	45mm	or	4.5cm	14	35.5	31	79	48	122
2	50mm	or	5cm	15	38	32	81.5	49	124.5
2½	65mm	or	6.5cm	16	40.5	33	84	50	127
3	75mm	or	7.5cm	17	43	34	86.5		
3½	90mm	or	9cm	18	46	35	89		
4	100mm	or	10cm	19	48.5	36	91.5		
4½	115mm	or	11.5cm	20	51	37	94		

YARDS TO METERS
(Slightly rounded off for convenience)

yards	meters	yards	meters	yards	meters	yards	meters	yards	meters
⅛	0.15	2⅛	1.95	4⅛	3.80	6⅛	5.60	8⅛	7.45
¼	0.25	2¼	2.10	4¼	3.90	6¼	5.75	8¼	7.55
⅜	0.35	2⅜	2.20	4⅜	4.00	6⅜	5.85	8⅜	7.70
½	0.50	2½	2.30	4½	4.15	6½	5.95	8½	7.80
⅝	0.60	2⅝	2.40	4⅝	4.25	6⅝	6.10	8⅝	7.90
¾	0.70	2¾	2.55	4¾	4.35	6¾	6.20	8¾	8.00
⅞	0.80	2⅞	2.65	4⅞	4.50	6⅞	6.30	8⅞	8.15
1	0.95	3	2.75	5	4.60	7	6.40	9	8.25
1⅛	1.05	3⅛	2.90	5⅛	4.70	7⅛	6.55	9⅛	8.35
1¼	1.15	3¼	3.00	5¼	4.80	7¼	6.65	9¼	8.50
1⅜	1.30	3⅜	3.10	5⅜	4.95	7⅜	6.75	9⅜	8.60
1½	1.40	3½	3.20	5½	5.05	7½	6.90	9½	8.70
1⅝	1.50	3⅝	3.35	5⅝	5.15	7⅝	7.00	9⅝	8.80
1¾	1.60	3¾	3.45	5¾	5.30	7¾	7.10	9¾	8.95
1⅞	1.75	3⅞	3.55	5⅞	5.40	7⅞	7.20	9⅞	9.05
2	1.85	4	3.70	6	5.50	8	7.35	10	9.15

AVAILABLE FABRIC WIDTHS

25″	65cm	50″	127cm
27″	70cm	54″/56″	140cm
35″/36″	90cm	58″/60″	150cm
39″	100cm	68″/70″	175cm
44″/45″	115cm	72″	180cm
48″	122cm		

AVAILABLE ZIPPER LENGTHS

4″	10cm	10″	25cm	22″	55cm
5″	12cm	12″	30cm	24″	60cm
6″	15cm	14″	35cm	26″	65cm
7″	18cm	16″	40cm	28″	70cm
8″	20cm	18″	45cm	30″	75cm
9″	22cm	20″	50cm		

Introduction

When my daughter was a little girl I gave her a dollhouse. As she avidly collected and made things for her tiny house, I too became fascinated with looking at the world in miniature. My lifelong love for crocheting and knitting naturally evolved into crocheting and knitting in miniature for my daughter's dollhouse. I found that with the correct needles, hooks and yarns I could create exquisite items for her house that could not be found anywhere! Now, my daughter's house cannot hold another item, and I wish to share my designs with other miniature enthusiasts. This book is a result of that desire.

Many of the designs are easy to execute, and require very little yarn, thread or floss to finish them. Also, when working in miniature, the projects take no time at all to complete! The projects are grouped in separate crochet and knitting sections, so pick the technique that suits your fancy. Full crochet and knitting directions are given with instructional diagrams to explain each technique and stitch. Photographs accompany each project to guide you as you work.

The most important aspect of crocheting and knitting in miniature is the yarn that you use. Pay careful attention to the yarn recommended for each project; if you are not familiar with that yarn, turn to the section entitled "Switchable Yarns." Look for your yarn in one of the five categories. You can substitute any yarns within a category, but do crochet or knit a test swatch with the appropriate hook or needles to make sure you have the correct gauge. Specific colors are listed for each project, but the colors are only suggestions. Use your imagination to create the color schemes that will best enhance your dollhouse and its furnishings.

How to Follow the Pattern Directions

ASTERISK (*): When an ★ appears, complete the directions immediately following it, and then repeat those directions across the entire row, or as many times as specified.

BRACKETS [ ]: When a series of directions is enclosed in brackets, work these directions the number of times specified, and then continue to work the rest of the row.

ITALICS: Useful hints and additional information—for example, the total number of stitches to be worked across a given row—are noted in italics. Recommended yarns are always noted in italics.

PARENTHESES ( ): Specific information and diagram letters and numbers are set off with parentheses.

WHIP-STITCH: To join two pieces together, such as pillows, take one loop from each piece and sew together following the diagram. Use matching yarn and small stitches for a professional result.

TASSELS: For each tassel, cut 3–4 lengths of yarn to double the length of the specified tassel. With the ends even, fold the yarn in half to form a loop. Insert a crochet hook from the wrong side into the stitch or space along the edge of the project to be fringed; insert hook through the loop of yarn, and pull the loop through the stitch or space in the project. Insert the cut ends of the tassel through the loop, then pull to tighten the knot. After all tassels have been added, trim evenly.

BLOCKING: Cut a piece of brown paper about 2″ larger all around than the finished size of your project. Using a pencil and ruler, mark the finished size (given at the beginning of each set of directions) in the center of the brown paper. Lay the paper on your ironing board; place the crocheted or knitted project, wrong side up, on the paper. Using the marked lines on the paper as a guide, tack the project to the ironing board with rustproof pins. If your piece was worked with synthetic yarns, dampen it and let it dry by itself; if you used wool or cotton yarn, lay a damp press cloth over the piece and press lightly with a steam iron.

Whip–Stitch Diagram

Crocheting for Dollhouses

How to Crochet

SLIP KNOT: Grasp the loose end of the yarn with your left hand and make an "O" with the yarn leading from the ball (the ball of yarn should be hanging behind the "O"). Pinch the top of the "O" between the thumb and middle finger of your left hand, and hold your crochet hook in your right hand as you would hold a pencil. Insert the tip of the hook and bring a loop from the yarn ball through the "O" (*A1*). Tighten the loop to complete the slip knot (*A2*). You are now ready to make your first chain stitch (the loop on your hook never counts when you are counting the stitches in your work).

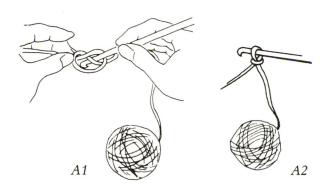

A1   *A2*

CHAIN STITCH: Pinch the base of the slip knot between the thumb and middle finger of your left hand, and wind the yarn from the ball over your forefinger. With the crochet hook inserted in the slip knot and the tip of the hook curved toward you, wrap the yarn around the hook from back to front (*B1*)—this is called a yarn over. Pull the yarn through the loop on the hook to complete the first chain stitch. Yarn over again and pull through the loop on the hook the number of times specified (*B2*). Each chain (and later each single crochet stitch) forms a distinct oval that can be clearly seen from the top of the work.

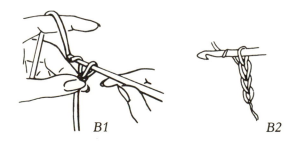

B1   *B2*

Counting the Chain Stitches: A loop is always on the hook when a stitch has been completed—just like the slip knot in the beginning. The loop on the hook is considered the beginning of each succeeding stitch, therefore it does not count as a stitch. In a row of chain stitches, the chain stitch immediately before the loop is the first stitch from the hook (*C*). The chain stitch preceeding that one is the second stitch from the hook and so on.

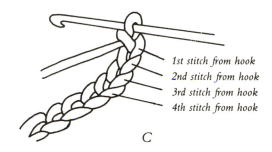

1st stitch from hook
2nd stitch from hook
3rd stitch from hook
4th stitch from hook

C

SLIP STITCH: Insert hook in a stitch, yarn over and then pull yarn through both the stitch and the loop on the hook in one motion (*D*). Slip stitch is similar to single crochet, but you do not yarn-over again before pulling the yarn through the loop on the hook.

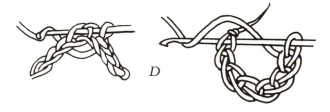

D

SINGLE CROCHET: Make a foundation chain of the required number of stitches (remember that the loop on the hook does not count as a stitch). Insert the hook in the second chain from the hook—the center of the oval (*E1*), yarn over and pull the loop through the stitch. You now have two loops on the hook (*E2*). Yarn over again (*E3*) and pull yarn through both loops on the hook to complete the first single crochet stitch (*E4*). Repeat until you have worked one single crochet stitch in each stitch of the foundation chain. Unless the pattern instructions specify otherwise, at the end of the first row and of each succeeding row, make one chain stitch (*E5*), and then turn the work so the yarn from the ball is once again at the right edge. For succeeding rows of single crochet, unless the instructions specifically tell you to do otherwise, always make the first stitch of a row in the last single crochet stitch of the previous row (not in the turning chain), and work each stitch by inserting the hook under both strands that form the oval of the stitch on the previous row (E6).

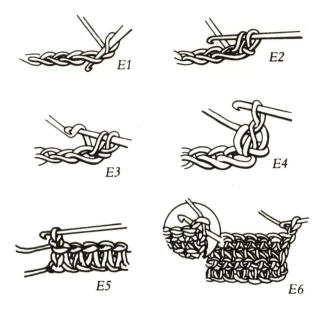

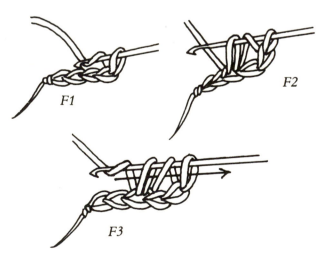

HALF DOUBLE CROCHET: Wrap the yarn over the hook and insert into the third chain from the hook (F1). Yarn over and draw through the chain—three loops on the hook (F2). Yarn over and draw through all three loops to complete the first half double crochet stitch (F3). Work a half double crochet in each chain across. At the end of the row, chain two and turn.

DOUBLE CROCHET: Wrap the yarn over the hook and insert into the fourth chain from the hook (G1). Yarn over and draw through the chain—three loops on the hook (G2). Yarn over and draw through the first two loops on the hook (G3). Yarn over and draw through the remaining two loops on the hook to complete the first double crochet (G4). When you have worked a double crochet in each chain across,

chain three and turn work. In most cases, the turning chain counts as the first double crochet of the next row. When working the second row, skip the first stitch and work a double crochet in the two top loops of each double crochet across. The last double crochet of each row is worked in the top chain of the turning chain.

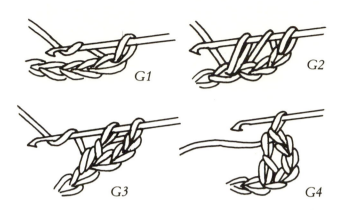

TREBLE OR TRIPLE CROCHET: Wrap the yarn twice over the hook and insert into the fifth chain from the hook. Yarn over and draw through the chain—four loops on hook (H). Yarn over and draw through two loops on hook, yarn over and draw through two more loops on hook, yarn over and draw through remaining two loops on hook to complete the first treble crochet. Work to the end of the row, chain four and turn; chain four counts as the first treble of the next row.

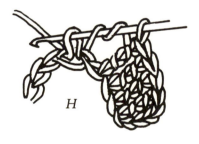

GAUGE: A crocheted fabric is measured by counting the number of stitches to the inch which gives the width measurement, and by counting the number of rows to the inch which gives the depth measurement. Always test your own gauge before beginning a project. To do this, chain 20, using the yarn and hook specified, and work in the pattern stitch for about 3″. Then measure how many stitches and rows you made per inch. If your swatch has more stitches and rows per inch than the number specified in the gauge, your work is too tight and you should use a larger crochet hook. If you have fewer stitches and rows per inch than the gauge, your work is too loose and you should switch to a smaller hook. *Note:* For projects where a gauge is not given, work with the yarn and hook specified.

INCREASING AND DECREASING: To increase one stitch, work two crochet stitches in the same stitch of the previous row.

To decrease one crochet stitch, work two stitches together in the following way: work the first stitch until the final yarn over, but do not yarn over; instead, begin to work the next stitch, working it also to the final yarn over; now yarn over and pull the yarn through all loops on the hook.

ATTACHING NEW YARN: If you run out of yarn or must add a new color in the course of working a piece, hold the new yarn against the wrong side of the work (this will always be the back of the piece unless the pattern instructions specifically indicate otherwise), leaving a loose 4″ end. Insert hook into the next stitch to be worked, yarn over and draw a loop of the new yarn through the stitch. Then finish the stitch and continue working in the usual manner, using the new yarn. Work the yarn ends into the backs of the next few stitches or, if you prefer, let them hang at the back of the work and weave them in later.

FASTENING OFF: Complete the last stitch of the piece and cut the yarn from the ball, leaving a 4″ yarn end. Then draw the yarn end through the remaining loop on the hook and pull tight. Thread the yarn end on a tapestry needle, weave it through the back of the work for about 1″, and trim the excess.

JOINING CROCHETED PIECES: Pin or hold the pieces together with the edges even. Thread a large-eyed needle with matching yarn, and work an overcast stitch through the loops of each pair of matching stitches. Sew through the inner loops only if you want to produce parallel lines on the front of the work (*J1*). Sew through the outer loops only if you want the parallel lines to appear on the reverse side of the work (*J2*).

 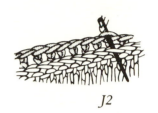

J1   *J2*

CROCHET ABBREVIATIONS

ch—chain	rnd—round
dc—double crochet	sc—single crochet
dec—decrease	sp—space
fs—fan stitch	ss—slip stitch
hdc—half double crochet	st, sts—stitch, stitches
inc—increase	tog—together
lp, lps—loop, loops	tr—treble crochet
pat—pattern	yo—yarn over
rep—repeat	

Petal Tablecloth

SIZE: About 6″ diameter.

MATERIALS: *(Belding Lily)* Daisy Mercerized Crochet Cotton No. 30, ecru. Steel crochet hook #10, or any size hook which will give the stitch gauge below.

GAUGE: 5 tr = ⅜″.

DIRECTIONS: Starting in center, ch 10, join with ss to form ring.

Rnd 1: Ch 3, 27 dc in ring, join with ss to top of third ch.

Rnd 2: Ch 5, ★ tr in next st, ch 1. Rep from ★ around (*27 tr*), join to fourth ch of ch 5.

Rnd 3: Ss in next sp, sc in same sp, ★ ch 4, sc in next sp. Rep from ★ around, join with ss to first ss.

Rnd 4: Ss to center of ch 4 lp, sc in same lp, ★ ch 4, sc in next ch 4 lp. Rep from ★ around, join with ss to first ss.

Rnd 5: Rep Rnd 4.

Rnd 6: Rep Rnd 4.

Rnd 7: Ss to center of next ch 4 lp, ch 4. Holding the last st of each tr back on hook, make 2 tr in same lp, yo and draw through all sts on hook (*cluster made*), ★ ch 6, sc in fourth ch from hook (*picot made*), ch 2, make a 3 tr cluster in next lp. Rep from ★ around, join to top of ch 4.

Rnd 8: Ss to center of next picot, ss in picot, ch 4, then work 4 tr in same picot, ★ ch 2, 5 tr in next picot. Rep from ★ around, join with ss to fourth ch.

Rnd 9: Ch 4, work 4 tr cluster over next 4 tr, ★ ch 7, sc in fourth ch from hook (*picot made*), ch 2, work a 5 tr cluster over the next 5 tr. Rep from ★ around, join to top of last cluster.

Rnd 10: Ss to center of next picot, ss in picot, ch 4, then work 2 tr cluster in same picot, ★ ch 7, sc in fourth ch from hook (*picot made*), ch 2, work a 3 tr cluster in next picot. Rep from ★ around, join with ss to top of cluster.

Rnd 11: Ss to center of next picot, ch 4, work 4 tr in same picot, ★ ch 3, 5 tr in next picot. Rep from ★ around, join with ss to fourth ch.

Rnd 12: Ch 4, ★ work 3 tr cluster over next 4 tr, ss over ch 3 to next tr, ch 4 in tr. Rep from ★ around. Fasten off. Block to measurement.

Lacy Tablecloth

SIZE: About 6″ diameter.

MATERIALS: *DMC Cordonnet Spécial #30,* white. Steel crochet hook #11.

GAUGE: 5 dc cluster = ¼″.

DIRECTIONS: Ch 10, join with ss to form ring.
Rnd 1: Ch 1, 24 sc in ring, ss to first sc.
Rnd 2: Ch 3, dc in next sc, [ch 3, dc in each of next 2 sc] 11 times, ch 3, ss to top of ch 3.
Rnd 3: Ss in first dc and in ch 3 sp, ch 1, sc in sp, [ch 4, sc in next sp] 11 times, ch 4, ss in first sc.
Rnd 4: Ss in first sp, ch 3, holding back on hook the last lp of each dc, work 4 dc in sp, yo and through all lps on hook (*cluster st made*), ch 5, 5 dc cluster in same sp, ★ ch 5, [5 dc cluster, ch 5, 5 dc cluster] once in next sp, ch 5. Rep from ★ around, ending ch 5, ss to top of first cluster (*19 ch 5 lps made*).
Rnd 5: Ss to center of first lp, ch 1, sc in sp, ch 5, sc in center of next sp. Rep from ★ around, ss in first ss (*19 lps made*).
Rnds 6–12: Rep Rnd 5, working ch quite loosely.
Rnd 13: Ch 1, work 7 sc in each ch 5 lp all around, join with ss to first sc.
Rnd 14: Ch 4, dc in next sc, ★ ch 1, skip 1 sc, 1 dc in next sc. Rep from ★ around. Ch 1, join with ss to third ch of first ch 4.
Rnd 15: Ss into next ch 1 sp, ch 1, sc in same sp, ★ ch 2, skip 1 ch 1 sp, in next sp work [2 dc, ch 3, 2 dc] once, ch 2, skip 1 ch 1 sp, sc in next sp. Rep from ★ around, ending ch 2, ss in first sc.
Rnd 16: ★ Ch 2, [2 dc, ch 3, 2 dc] once in next ch 3 sp, ch 2, sc in next sc. Rep from ★ around.
Rnd 17: Rep Rnd 16, working ch 3 instead of ch 2. Fasten off. Block to measurement.

Granny's Kitchen Mat

SIZE: About 6″ square.

MATERIALS: *Pingouin fil d'écosse No. 5,* sable. Or for a coarse texture, small ball of linen yarn. Steel crochet hook #3. Large-eyed needle.

GAUGE: 3 dc = ⅜″; first rnd = ⅞″ square.

DIRECTIONS: Make 4 squares as follows: Starting in center, ch 4, join with ss to form ring.
Rnd 1: Ch 3, 2 dc in ring, [ch 3, 3 dc in ring] 3 times. Ch 3, ss to top of first ch 3.
Rnd 2: Ss to next ch 3 corner sp, ch 3, 2 dc, ch 3, 3 dc in same sp. ★ Ch 1, 3 dc, ch 3, 3 dc in next corner sp. Rep from ★ twice more. Ch 1, ss to top of first ch 3.

Rnd 3: Ss to next ch 3 corner sp, ch 3, 2 dc, ch 3, 3 dc in same sp. ★ Ch 1, 3 dc in ch 1 sp, ch 1, 3 dc, ch 3, 3 dc in next corner sp. Rep from ★ twice more. Ch 1, 3 dc in next ch 1 sp, ch 1, ss to top of first ch 3.
Rnd 4: Ss to next ch 3 corner sp, ch 3, 2 dc, ch 3, 3 dc in same sp. ★ [3 dc in next ch 1 sp] twice, 3 dc, ch 3, 3 dc in next corner sp. Rep from ★ twice more. [3 dc in next ch 1 sp] twice, ss to top of first ch 3. Fasten off.

Finishing: Sew 4 squares tog through back lps only to form a square.

Edging: Dc in each dc around, working 3 dc, ch 3, 3 dc in each corner sp, and 1 dc where squares are joined. Fasten off. Press flat.

Oval Dining Room Rug

SIZE: About 5¼" × 7".

MATERIALS: *Bernat® Cassino® Mercerized Cotton*, 1 50 gram ball each, geranium and black. Steel crochet hook #2, or any size hook which will give the stitch gauge below.

GAUGE: Using 2 strands, 7 sc = 1".

DIRECTIONS: Work with 2 strands of *Cassino* throughout. Starting with geranium in center, ch 12.
Rnd 1: Sc in second ch from hook and in each ch across to within last ch, work 3 sc in last ch. Continue to sc along other edge of ch to within last ch, work 3 sc in last ch.
Rnd 2: Sc in each sc of previous rnd; inc evenly at each end of oval to keep work flat (*to inc, work 2 or 3 sc in 1 sc as necessary*).
Rnds 3–4: Rep Rnd 2. Fasten off geranium; attach black.
Rnds 5–7: Rep Rnd 2. Join with ss at end of Rnd 7.
Rnd 8: Ch 3, dc in each sc around, inc evenly as necessary to keep work flat, join with ss at end. Fasten off black.
Rnd 9: Attach geranium. Ch 3, work dc in each dc of previous rnd, inc evenly all around as necessary. Join with ss at end. Fasten off geranium.
Rnds 10–11: Attach black. Ch 3, work dc in each dc of previous rnd, inc evenly all around. Join with ss at end of Rnd 11. Fasten off black.
Rnd 12: Rep Rnd 9. Press flat.

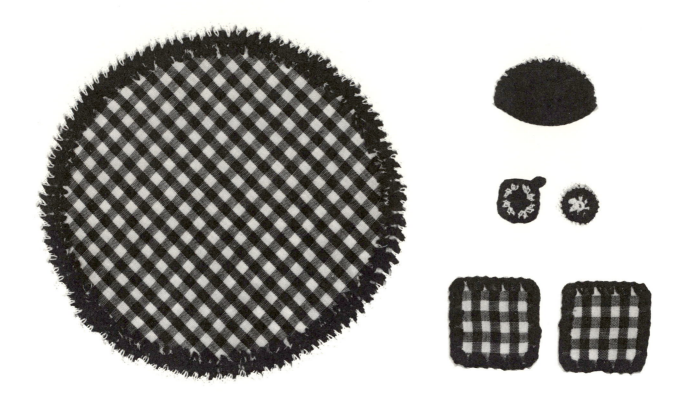

Gingham Kitchen Set

SIZES: See individual directions.

MATERIALS: Gingham with ⅛″ checks, red and white, ¼ yard. *DMC Pearl Cotton #8,* 1 ball each: red, white. Steel crochet hook #11. Sewing needle. Scissors. Compass. Iron. Thread.

DIRECTIONS: Tablecloth (*5½″ diameter*): Use a compass to mark a 5″-diameter circle on gingham; cut out on marked line. Attach red with ss to raw edge of fabric.

Rnd 1: Sc, ch 1 evenly all around raw edge of fabric; join with ss (*about 104 sc*).

Rnd 2: Ch 4, sc in each ch 1 sp all around, join with ss. Break off red. Attach white to any ch 1 sp.

Rnd 3: Ch 4, sc in next ch 1 sp all around to make loops, join with ss. Fasten off. Press flat.

Curtains (*About 3¼″ × 5½″*): Cut 2 rectangles of gingham, each 3″ × 5″. With ss, attach red ¾″ from beg of 1 long edge of 1 piece.

Rnd 1: Sc, ch 1 along 1 long edge (*about 33 sc*). Sc, ch 1, sc, ch 1, sc in corner. Sc, ch 1 along short edge (*about 15 sc*). Work second corner as for first, then work second long edge as for first, finishing ¾″ from top edge. Turn.

Rnd 2: Ch 4, sc in ch 1 sp along 1 long side and 1 short side. Fasten off red. Attach white to first red ch 4 loop.

Rnd 3: Ch 4, sc in ch 4 loop along 1 long and 1 short side. Fasten off.

Press ¾″ raw edge ⅜″ to wrong side of curtain twice, making ⅜″ hem; slip-stitch in place with matching thread. Rep for second curtain, working Rnds 2–3 along opposite edges from those on first curtain.

Valence (*About 4¼″ × 1¼″*): Cut 4″ × 1″ rectangle of gingham. With ss, attach red to corner of 1 long edge.

Rnd 1: ★ Sc, ch 1 evenly along 1 long edge (*about 28 sc*). Sc, ch 1, sc, ch 1, sc in corner. Sc, ch 1 along short edge (*3 sc*). Work second corner as for first. Rep from ★ around to work second long and short edges and corners.

Rnd 2: Ch 4, sc in ch 1 sp along 1 long edge. Break off red and attach white to first red ch 4 loop.

Rnd 3: Ch 4, sc in ch 4 loop all across. Fasten off.

Napkins (*About 1¼″ square*): Cut 2 pieces of gingham, each 1¼″ square. With ss, attach red to corner of 1 piece. Sc, ch 1 evenly along 1 edge (*6 sc*). Work 3 sc in corner, then rep for all other edges. Fasten off. Make second napkin same as for first.

Tea Cozy (*About 1½″ × 1″*): **Front:** With red, ch 22.

Row 1: Dc in fourth ch from hook and in each ch across, ch 3, turn (*18 dc*).

Rows 2–3: Skip first dc (*ch 3 counts as first dc*), dc in each dc across, ending with dc in top of turning ch, ch 3, turn.

Row 4 (*Dec row*): Skip first dc, ★ [yo, pull up loop in next st, yo, pull through 2 loops] twice; yo, pull through 3 loops on hook (*1 dc dec*). Rep from ★ across row, ending with dc in top of turning ch, ch 3, turn.

Row 5: Rep Row 4, ending with ss in top of turning ch. Fasten off.

Back: Work same as for front.

Finishing: Using white, sc front and back tog around curved edges, leaving bottom edge open; work a ch 7 loop at center top.

Granny Square Pot Holder (*½″ square*): Starting in center with red, ch 4, join with ss to form ring.

Rnd 1: Ch 2, 1 hdc in ring, [ch 2, 2 hdc in ring] 3 times, ch 2, ss to top of first ch 2. Fasten off.

Rnd 2: Attach white to 1 ch 2 corner sp. [2 hdc, ch 2, 2 hdc] in each ch 2 corner sp, join with ss. Fasten off.

Rnd 3: With red, sc in each dc around, working 3 sc in 3 corner sp, and 1 sc, ch 6, 1 sc in 1 corner sp, join with ss. Fasten off.

Round Pot Holder (*½″ diameter*): Starting in center with white, ch 6, join with ss to form ring.

Rnd 1: Work 12 sc in ring, join with ss.

Rnd 2: Ch 2, hdc in ss. Work 2 hdc in each sc around, join with ss (*25 hdc*). Fasten off.

Rnd 3: With red, sc in a hdc, ★ work 1 hdc, inserting hook at base of next hdc on previous row, sc in next hdc. Rep from ★ around, join with ss. Fasten off.

Rnd 4: With white, sc in each st around, working a ch 6 loop in 1 st, join with ss. Fasten off.

Bathroom Set

SIZES: Bath mat, 2½″ diameter. Towel, 2¾″ × 1⅜″. Wash cloth, ¾″ square.

MATERIALS: Scraps of lightweight stretch velour, desired color. *(Belding) Lily Tatting Crochet,* in color to match or contrast with velour. Steel crochet hook #12. Compass. Ruler. Paper for patterns.

DIRECTIONS: Bath Mat: Use compass to mark a 2″-diameter circle on paper. Use paper pattern to cut circle of stretch velour. Using tatting crochet cotton, sc around raw edge *(62 sc)*; join with ss.
Next Rnd: Ch 3, work 2 dc in same sc, ch 3, ss in second ch from hook *(picot made)*. ★ Skip 1 sc, 3 dc in next sc, ch 3, ss in second ch from hook. Rep from ★ around; ss to top of ch 3. Fasten off. Press flat.

Towel: Use ruler to mark 1¼″ × 2½″ pattern on paper; use pattern to cut 1 piece from velour. Using tatting crochet cotton, work 2 rnds sc around raw edges, working 3 sc in each corner. Fasten off. Attach cotton in right corner of 1 short edge: ch 4, skip 1 sc, dc in next sc, ★ ch 1, skip 1 sc, dc in next sc. Rep from ★ across. Ch 1, turn. Sc in each st across. Fasten off. Press flat.

Wash Cloth: Use ruler to mark ¾″ square pattern on paper; use pattern to cut 1 piece from velour. Using tatting crochet cotton, work 2 rnds sc around raw edges, working 3 sc in each corner. On the final corner, ch 8; join with ss and fasten off *(the ch 8 forms the loop to hang the cloth)*. Press flat.

Oval Rug

SIZE: About 2¾″ × 3¾″.

MATERIALS: *Brunswick Brunsana® Persian Yarn,* 1 8.8 yd. skein each: faded beige, summer blue, dark maroon, dark brown. Steel crochet hook #7, or any size hook which will give the stitch gauge below.

GAUGE: 5 sc = ½″; 5 rows = ½″ *(using a single strand of yarn)*.

DIRECTIONS: Separate yarn into 3 strands; work with 1 strand throughout. Starting with blue in center, ch 12.
Rnd 1: Sc in second ch from hook and in each ch across to within last ch, work 2 sc in last ch. Continue to sc along other edge of ch to within last ch, work 2 sc in last ch.
Rnd 2: Sc in each sc of previous rnd; work 2 sc in each sc before and after sc at each end *(4 sts inc)*. Fasten off. Attach beige.
Rnd 3: Sc all around, working 3 sc at each end of oval.
Rnds 4–5: Rep Rnd 3. Fasten off beige at end of Rnd 5.
Rnds 6–8: Attach maroon; rep Rnd 3. Fasten off maroon at end of Rnd 8.
Rnds 9–11: Attach beige; rep Rnd 3. Fasten off beige at end of Rnd 11.
Rnds 12–14: Attach brown; rep Rnd 3. Fasten off brown at end of Rnd 14. Press flat.

Picot Rug

SIZE: About 3″ × 4½″.

MATERIALS: *Bernat® Berella® 3-Ply Fingering,* one skein each of white and rose heather. Crochet hook, size D, or any size hook which will give the stitch gauge below.

GAUGE: 6 sc = 1″.

DIRECTIONS: Starting in center with white, ch 8.

Rnd 1: Sc in second ch from hook and in each ch across to within last ch, work 3 sc in last ch. Continue to sc along other edge of ch to within last ch, work 3 sc in last ch.

Rnd 2: Sc all around, working 3 sc at each end of oval; fasten off white.

Rnds 3–6: Attach rose, work as for Rnd 2; fasten off rose at end of Rnd 6.

Rnds 7–8: Attach white, work as for Rnd 2; fasten off white at end of Rnd 8.

Picot Edging: Attach rose to any sc. ★ Ch 3, ss in second ch from hook (*picot made*), skip 1 sc, sc in next sc. Rep from ★ around. Join ends and fasten off. Press flat.

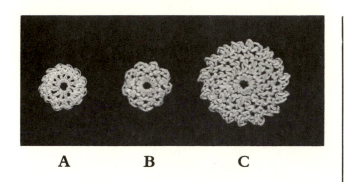

A   **B**   **C**

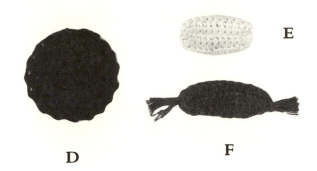

D   **F**

Petal Doily

SIZE: ¾″ diameter.

MATERIALS: *DMC Cébélia Size 30,* white. Steel crochet hook #11.

DIRECTIONS: (A) Ch 6, join with ss to form ring.
Rnd 1: Ch 4, ★ dc in ring, ch 1. Rep from ★ 10 times. Join with ss to third ch of first ch 4.
Rnd 2: Ss to center of next ch 1 space, ★ sc, 2 dc, sc in same space. Rep from ★ 10 times. Fasten off.

Ecru Doilies

SIZE: Small, ¾″ diameter. Large, 1¼″ diameter.

MATERIALS: For Both: *J. & P. Coats "Knit-Cro-Sheen,"* ecru. Steel crochet hook #3.

DIRECTIONS: Small Doily: (B) With cotton, ch 5, join with ss to form ring.
Rnd 1: Ch 1, work 8 sc in ring.
Rnd 2: ★ Ch 3, ss in next sc. Rep from ★ around. Fasten off.

Large Doily: (C) With cotton, ch 5, join with ss to form ring.
Rnd 1: Ch 1, work 8 sc in ring.
Rnd 2: Ch 3, dc in same sc, ★ 1 dc in next sc, 2 dc in next sc. Continue from ★ around, ending 1 dc in next sc. Join with ss (*12 dc*).
Rnd 3: ★ Ch 3, ss in second ch from hook, 1 sc in next dc. Rep from ★ around. Fasten off.

Circular Pillow

SIZE: About 1¼″ diameter.

MATERIALS: *Bernat® Cassino® Mercerized Cotton,* red. Steel crochet hook #1. Stuffing.

DIRECTIONS: (D) Ch 5, join with ss to form ring.
Rnd 1: Ch 1, 7 sc in ring, join with ss.
Rnd 2: Ch 2, 2 dc in each sc around, join with ss. Fasten off. Make 2 circles.

Join circles tog with sc, being sure to stuff pillow before closing opening completely.

Bolster Pillows

SIZE: Fringed pillow, about 1¼″ long without fringe. Small pillow, about 1″ long.

MATERIALS: *J. & P. Coats Deluxe Six Strand Floss,* one skein beauty rose. *J. & P. Coats Six Cord Mercerized #30,* white. Steel crochet hooks #9 and #11. Cotton balls.

DIRECTIONS: Fringed Pillow: (F) With #9 hook and 6-strand floss, ch 13.
Row 1: Sc in second ch from hook, sc to end, ch 1, turn.
Row 2: Sc in *back* of each st of the previous row, ch 1, turn.

Rep Row 2 until piece measures 1″. Roll into bolster shape; sew long edges tog. Stuff with cotton; sew short ends closed. Attach a ¼″ fringe at each end.

Small Pillow: (E) Work as for fringed pillow using a #11 crochet hook and #30 cotton. Do not attach fringe.

Rainbow Afghan

SIZE: 4¼″ square without tassels.

MATERIALS: *Susan Bates Anchor® Stranded Cotton,* 1 skein each of the following: (A) canary yellow dk., (B) melon dk., (C) crimson, (D) emerald med., (E) ice blue med., (F) wedgewood dk. Steel crochet hook #11 or any size hook which will give the stitch gauge below.

GAUGE: First round = 1 ⅛″ square.

DIRECTIONS: Starting in center with A, ch 6, join with ss to form ring.
Rnd 1: Ch 3, in ring work 3 dc, ch 2, [4 dc, ch 2] 3 times, join with ss to top of starting ch. Fasten off.
Rnd 2: Attach color B to any ch 2 sp, ch 3, in same sp work 3 dc, ch 2, 4 dc, [ch 1, in next sp work 4 dc, ch 2, 4 dc] 3 times, ch 1, join with ss to top of starting ch. Fasten off.
Rnd 3: Attach color C to any ch 2 sp, ch 3, in same sp work 3 dc, ch 2, 4 dc, [ch 1, in next ch 1 sp work 4 dc, ch 1, in next corner sp work 4 dc, ch 3, 4 dc] 3 times, ch 1, 4 dc in last ch 1 sp, ch 1, join with ss to top of starting ch. Fasten off.

Continue in this manner, working each round in the following color sequence: D, E, F, A, B, C. You will end with 7 dc sets in between each corner on the last rnd.

Attach a red tassel, ¼″ long, in each corner, and a variety of colored ¼″ tassels in each ch 1 sp around entire afghan.

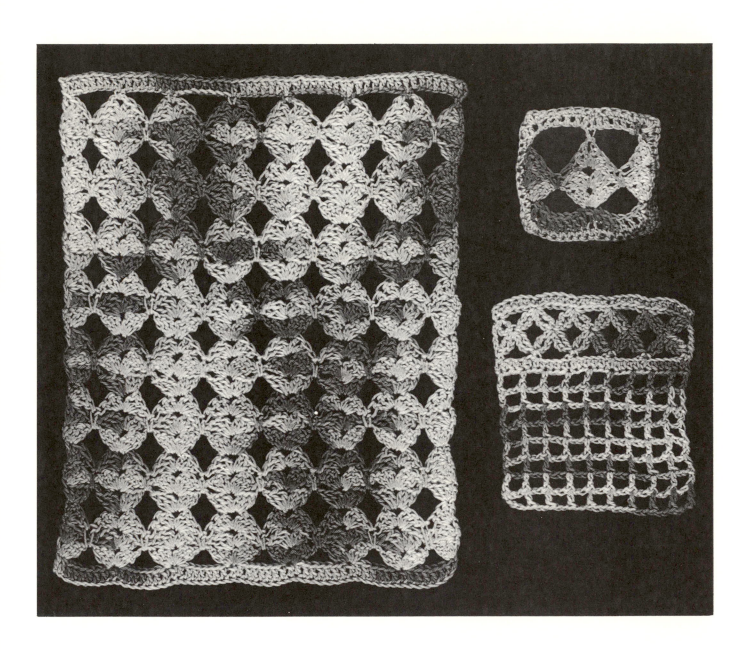

Variegated Bedroom Set

SIZES: See individual directions.

MATERIALS: *J. & P. Coats "Knit-Cro-Sheen,"* 1 ball shaded blues #13. Steel crochet hook #3, or any size hook which will give the stitch gauge below.
For Pillow: 2 pieces blue felt, each 2″ square. Stuffing.

GAUGE: 1 fs = ⅞″ wide.

NOTE: 1 fan stitch (fs) = 3 dc, ch 2, 3 dc all worked into the same stitch or space.

DIRECTIONS: Bedspread (6½″ × 8″): Ch 58. Work 1 dc in third ch from hook, dc in each ch across, ch 3, turn. Work in pat as follows:
Row 1: 3 dc in first st, ch 2, ★ skip 7 sts, 1 fs in next st, ch 2. Rep from ★, ending 4 dc in top of turning ch, ch 3, turn.
Row 2: 3 dc in first st, ch 2, ★ 1 fs in ch 2 sp of next fs, ch 2. Rep from ★, ending 4 dc in top of turning ch, ch 3, turn.
Row 3: 3 dc in first st, ★ 1 sc over *both* ch 2 bars of 2 previous rows, 1 fs in next ch 2 sp at center of next fs. Rep from ★, ending 4 dc in top of turning ch, ch 3, turn.
Row 4: Rep Row 2.
Row 5: Rep Row 2.
Row 6: Rep Row 3.
Continue working Rows 2–6, making 8 complete motifs.
Next Row: [Ch 7, sc in ch 2 sp of fs] 6 times across row, ch 7, sc in top of turning ch, ch 3, turn.
Last Row: Work 1 dc in each ch across. Fasten off.

Pillow (*about 2″ square*): Ch 18. Work 1 dc in third ch from hook, dc in each ch across, ch 3, turn. Work 1 full pat (6 rows) following *Bedspread* directions.
Next Row: Ch 7, sc in ch 2 sp of fs, ch 7, sc in top of turning ch, ch 3, turn.
Last Row: Work 1 dc in each ch across. Fasten off.

Make second piece in same manner. Sew felt pieces tog around edges; stuff before sewing fourth side closed. With wrong sides facing, join crocheted pieces along 3 sides with sc. Insert blue felt pillow, sc fourth side closed.

Curtain (*about 3″ × 3½″*): **Gauge:** 6 leaves = 2″. Ch 27. Work 1 hdc in third ch from hook, 1 hdc in each ch to end, ch 3, turn. Work in leaf pat as follows:
Row 1: 1 tr in first hdc, ★ skip 4 sts, 1 tr in next hdc, ch 3, ss in same hdc, ch 3, 1 tr in same hdc. Rep from ★, ending skip 4 sts, 1 tr in last hdc, ch 3, ss in same hdc, ch 5, turn.
Row 2: ★ In st between next 2 leaves, work 1 tr, ch 3, ss in same st, ch 3, 1 tr in same st. Rep from ★, ending 1 tr into top of turning ch on previous row, ch 1, turn.
Row 3: 1 sc into first st, ★ ch 4, 1 sc in st between 2 leaves. Rep from ★ across, ending ch 4, 1 sc in last leaf, ch 2, turn.
Row 4: Work 1 hdc in each st across, ch 4, turn.
Row 5: ★ Skip 2 sts, 1 dc in next st, ch 2. Rep from ★, ending skip 1 st, 1 dc in next st, ch 4, turn.
Row 6: ★ 1 dc in top of last dc, ch 2. Rep from ★ across, ending 1 dc in center of ch 4, ch 4, turn.

Rep Row 6 until curtain measures 3½″ or desired length. Fasten off.

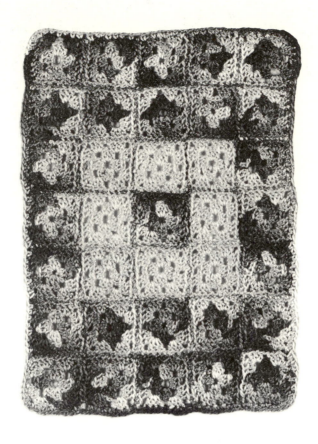

Granny Square Afghan

SIZE: 4″ × 5½″.

MATERIALS: *DMC Pearl Cotton #8,* 1 ball each of (*A*) yellow #445, and (*B*) variegated blue #113, or desired colors. Steel crochet hook #11. Large-eyed needle.

DIRECTIONS: Make each granny square as follows: Starting at center with color A, ch 6, join with ss to form ring.
Rnd 1: Ch 3, 2 dc in ring, ch 3, [3 dc in ring, ch 3] 3 times. Join with ss to top of starting ch 3.
Rnd 2: Ss in next 2 dc, ss in next sp, [ch 3, 2 dc, ch 3, 3 dc] once in same sp, ★ ch 1, [3 dc, ch 3, 3 dc] once in next sp. Rep from ★ twice more. Ch 1, join with ss to top of starting ch 3. Fasten off.

Make 8 granny squares with *A* and 27 squares with *B*. Sew squares tog following diagram. Press flat.

Note: To make a matching pillow, make 2 squares. Sew tog on 3 sides, stuff, then sew fourth side closed. Sc, 2 dc, sc all around for a scalloped edge, if desired.

B	B	B	B	B
B	B	B	B	B
B	A	A	A	B
B	A	B	A	B
B	A	A	A	B
B	B	B	B	B
B	B	B	B	B

Granny Square Afghan Diagram

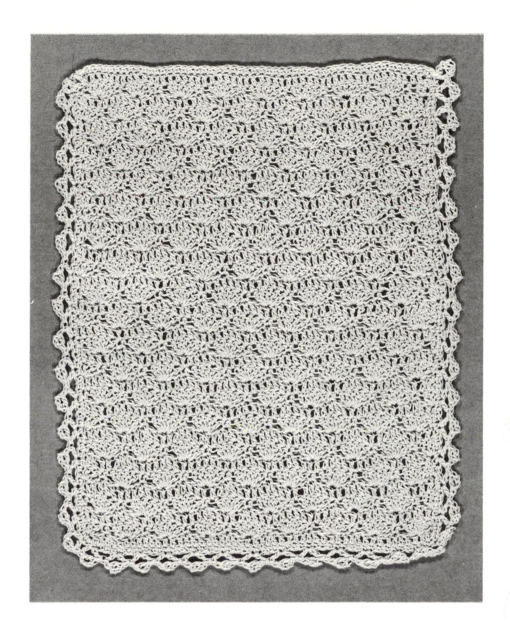

Shell Bedspread

SIZE: Bedspread, 5¾" × 7¼".

MATERIALS: *DMC Cébélia Size 20,* 1 ball ecru. Steel crochet hook #7, or any size hook which will give the stitch gauge below.

GAUGE: 1 shell = ⅜".

DIRECTIONS: Ch 55. Work in shell pat as follows:
Row 1: Dc in fourth ch from hook and in each ch across, ch 1, turn.
Row 2: Sc in first dc, ★ skip 2 dc, 5 dc in next dc, skip 2 dc, sc in next dc. Rep from ★, ending with 2 dc in last dc, ch 3, turn.

Row 3: Dc in each st across, ch 3, turn.
Row 4: 2 dc in first dc, ★ skip 2 dc, sc in next dc, skip 2 dc, 5 dc in next dc. Rep from ★, ending with sc in last dc, ch 3, turn.

Row 5: Dc in each st across, ch 1, turn.

Rep Rows 2–5 until 37 rows are completed, ending with Row 3 or 5; do not fasten off. Work a round of sc along all 4 sides of bedspread, working 3 sc in each corner.

Making edging as follows: Ch 7, dc in fourth ch from hook, dc in same sc where ch 7 began, ★ skip 3 sc, dc in next sc, ch 4, dc in fourth ch from hook, dc in same sc. Rep from ★ along 2 long sides and 1 short side of bedspread. Fasten off.

Heirloom Bedspread

SIZE: 5½″ × 7¼″ without fringe.

MATERIALS: *Susan Bates® Fashion-Tone™ Mercerized Cotton,* cream. Steel crochet hook #4, or any size hook which will give the stitch gauge below.

GAUGE: 4 dc = ½″.

DIRECTIONS: Ch 58. **Row 1:** 1 dc in fourth ch from hook, ★ skip 2 ch, [1 dc, ch 3, 1 dc] once in next st, skip 1 ch, 1 dc in each of next 4 ch. Rep from ★ ending 1 dc in each of last 2 ch. Ch 3, turn.

Row 2: 1 dc in next st, ★ [ch 1, 1 dc, ch 3, 1 dc, ch 1] once in next ch 3 sp, skip next st, 1 dc in each of next 4 sts. Rep from ★ ending 1 dc in last dc and in top of ch 3. Ch 3, turn.

Row 3: 1 dc in next st, ★ [ch 1, 1 dc, ch 3, 1 dc, ch 1] once in next ch 3 sp, skip next ch 1 sp, 1 dc in each of next 4 sts. Rep from ★ ending 1 dc in last dc and in top of ch 3. Ch 3, turn.

Row 3 forms the pat. Rep Row 3 until piece measures 5¼″ or desired width. Fasten off. Using 2 strands for each, make 80 tassels, each ½″ long, and attach around 2 long sides and 1 short side. Trim evenly.

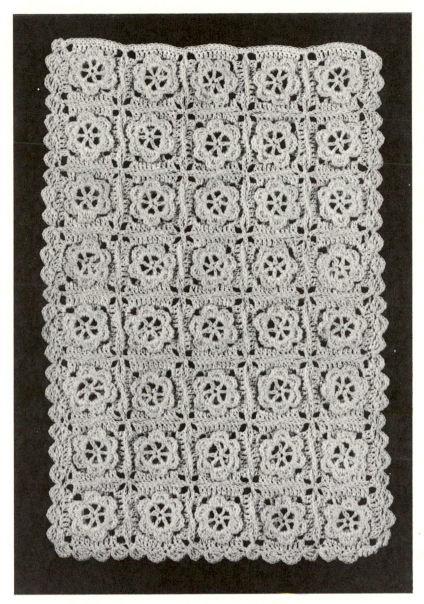

Rose Bedspread

SIZE: 5¼″ × 8¼″.

MATERIALS: *J. & P. Coats "Knit-Cro-Sheen,"* 1 ball white. Steel crochet hook #11. Large-eyed needle.

GAUGE: Each motif = 1″ square.

DIRECTIONS: (*Make 40 motifs.*) Starting in center of motif, ch 5, join with ss to form ring.
Rnd 1: Ch 5, dc in ring, [ch 2, dc in ring] 4 times, ch 2, join to third ch of ch 5.
Rnd 2: Work 1 sc, 4 dc, 1 sc in each ch 2 sp around (*6 petals made*).
Rnd 3: Ss *behind* petals to base of dc's in Rnd 2. Work 4 ch 5 lps in base of dc's, evenly divided behind petals. Ch 3.

Rnd 4: In each ch 5 lp, work 6 dc (*ch 3 counts as first dc*), ch 2 for each corner; end ch 2, join with ss to top of ch 3.
Rnd 5: Ch 3, dc in each of next 5 dc, ★ 2 dc, ch 3, 2 dc in ch 2 corner sp, 1 dc in each of next 6 dc. Rep from ★ around, ending 2 dc, ch 3, 2 dc in corner sp, join to top of ch 3. Fasten off.

Assembly: Sew motifs tog through back lps only, making 8 rows with 5 squares in each row.

Edging: (*Work along 2 long sides and 1 short side.*) Attach cotton to one ch 3 corner sp, sc in corner sp, ch 3, 3 dc in same sp, ★ skip ¼″ of edge, work [sc, ch 3, 3 dc] once in edge. Rep from ★ around 3 sides. Sc evenly along remaining short side. Fasten off.

Knitting for Dollhouses

How to Knit

CASTING ON: First Loop: Wind the yarn twice around the first 2 fingers (*A1*). Insert one needle in the back loop (*A2*). Draw the yarn through the center opening and tighten for the first loop or stitch (*A3*). Next, cast on the required number of stitches, choosing the method below, or your favorite method.

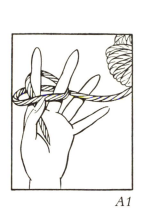

Continental Single Cast-On: Hold 2 needles together in the right hand; this opens the loops considerably, and makes knitting the first row easier. It also adds elasticity to the edge. Make the first loop around 2 needles, then loop the yarn around the thumb and third finger as shown (*B*). Add the stitches by inserting the needles upward through the loop on the thumb following the arrow. After the required number of stitches have been cast on, withdraw *one* of the needles.

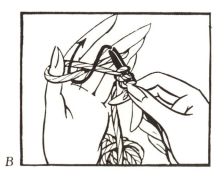

KNIT STITCH: Hold the needle containing the cast-on loops in the left hand; insert the right needle into the front of the next stitch to be worked (*C1*).

Draw the working yarn under the right needle and through to the front as a new loop (*C2*), then slip the old stitch off the left needle.

PURL STITCH: With the yarn to the front of the fabric, insert the right needle into the front of the next stitch to be worked (*D1*). Loop the working yarn over and under the point of the needle, and draw the right needle and loop just made through the stitch (*D2*), then slip the old stitch off the left needle.

GARTER STITCH: When the knit stitch is worked every row on 2 needles, the surface of the resulting fabric is "rough," giving the impression of purl knitting (*E*).

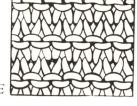

STOCKINETTE STITCH: When 1 row is knitted, and the next row is worked in purl stitch on 2 needles, the surface of the resulting fabric is "smooth," and provides a vertical line of design which resembles a chain (*F*).

SEED STITCH: When the odd rows are worked in knit one, purl one, and the even rows are worked with a purl stitch over a knit stitch and a knit stitch over a purl stitch, the surface of the resulting fabric is "textured," giving the impression of evenly staggered knots (G).

G

GAUGE: A knitted fabric is measured by counting the number of stitches to the inch which gives the width measurement, and by counting the number of rows to the inch which gives the depth measurement (H). Always test your own gauge before beginning a project. To do this, cast on approximately 20 stitches, using the yarn and needle size specified, and work in the pattern stitch specified for about 3". Then measure how many stitches and rows you made per inch. If your swatch has more stitches and rows per inch than the gauge called for in the project instructions, your work is too tight and you should use larger knitting needles; if you have fewer stitches and rows per inch than the project gauge, your work is too loose and you should change to smaller knitting needles. *Note:* For projects where a gauge is not given, work with the yarn and needles specified; in this case, gauge is not essential to the finished project.

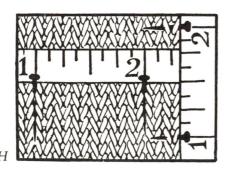

H

INCREASING: Single Invisible Increase: Knit first into the front of the stitch and form one loop as shown, then knit into the back of the same stitch (I) to form a second loop. Slip both loops off together and the extra stitch is made. On the next row, knit or purl this extra loop as an ordinary stitch.

I

DECREASING: Knit 2 Together (K 2 tog): Insert the right needle knitwise through 2 stitches and knit them together as 1 stitch (J). *A single decrease has been made.*

J

Slip 1, Knit 1, Pass Slip-Stitch Over (s1 1, K 1, psso): Slip 1 stitch from the left to the right needle. Insert the right needle knitwise through the next stitch (K1), and knit it. Next, insert the left needle through the stitch previously slipped (K2), and draw this over the knitted stitch following the arrow. *A single decrease has been made.*

K1 K2

Purl 2 Together (P 2 tog): Insert the right needle purlwise through 2 stitches, and purl them together as 1 stitch (L). *A single decrease has been made.*

L

Slip 1, Knit 2 Together, Pass Slip-Stitch Over (s1 1, K 2 tog, psso): Slip 1 stitch and knit the next 2 stitches together (M1). Insert the left needle through the slipped stitch and draw it over the knitted stitch (M2). *A double decrease has been made.*

M1 M2

Slip-Slip-Knit (ssk): Slip 2 stitches, then knit the next stitch. Lift both slipped stitches over the knitted stitch. *A double decrease has been made.*

YARN OVER: Knit Row: With the yarn forward, as if to purl, wrap the yarn over the needle, then knit the next stitch (N). On the return row, the over is treated as a stitch and knitted or purled in the same way as the other stitches. A yarn over is an increase stitch. To make a yarn over stitch without increasing the total number of stitches, knit two together before or after the over.

N

Purl Row: With the yarn forward as if to purl, wrap the yarn over and around the needle, then purl the next stitch (*O*). Purl two together if you wish to make a yarn over without increasing the total number of stitches in a row.

O

USING A DOUBLE POINTED NEEDLE: When two or more stitches cross over one another in pairs or threes, they cannot be knitted, but must be crossed (*P1* and *P3*). *The figures show units of three, but larger units or units of two are made in the same way.*

Cable Back (*CB*): Slip two or three stitches on a double pointed needle, and hold in back of the work. Knit stitches A, B and C, then knit stitches D, E and F off the double pointed needle. Figure *P2* shows the result of a cable back.

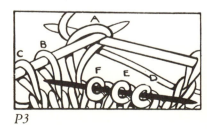

P1

P2

Cable Front (*CF*): Slip two or three stitches on a double pointed needle and hold in the front of the work. Knit stitches A, B and C, then knit stitches D, E and F off the double pointed needle. Figure *P4* shows the result of a cable front.

P3

P4

COLOR KNITTING: When colored patterns are worked in stockinette stitch, always twist the different color yarns where they meet to avoid gaps in the work. When working a pattern, the yarn not in use should be stranded across the back of the work. When the yarn has to be stranded over more than 5 stitches, twist the strand around the yarn in use on every third stitch to prevent long strands on the back of the work.

CASTING OFF: Knit the first 2 stitches, then draw the first stitch over the second and off the needle (*Q*). Knit a third stitch and draw the second knitted stitch over the third; repeat until the last stitch has been reached. Cut the yarn, leaving a 3″ length, and draw through the last stitch; tighten to fasten securely.

This method, though widely used, does not leave an elastic edge, and will probably tighten the knitted piece. Using a large needle (*2 sizes larger*) in the right hand will safeguard against excessive tightening.

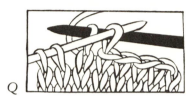

Q

WEAVE TOGETHER: To weave two pieces together, thread a large-eyed needle with matching yarn and pick up the end loops from each row alternately from side to side (*R*). Pull yarn lightly to draw the pieces together snugly.

R

KNITTING ABBREVIATIONS

beg—beginning	psso—pass slip-stitch
CB—cable back	over
CF—cable front	rep—repeat
dec—decrease	SDS—seed stitch
dp—double pointed	sl—slip
GS—garter stitch	SS—stockinette stitch
inc—increase	ssk—slip, slip, knit
K—knit	st, sts—stitch, stitches
lp—loop	tog—together
P—purl	yo—yarn over
pat—pattern	

Welcome Mat

SIZE: 2¼″ × 4″.

MATERIALS: *DMC Pearl Cotton #3,* 1 skein each, light beige and dark brown. #1 knitting needles, or any needles which will give the stitch gauge below.

GAUGE: 17 sts = 2¼″; 10 rows = 1″ *(blocked).*

DIRECTIONS: With dark brown, cast on 17 sts. Work 2 rows in SDS. Following pat on chart and working the first 2 and last 2 sts of every row in SDS, work mat in SS, knitting "Welcome" in light beige. Work the last 2 rows in SDS. Cast off. Block to measurements.

Doll Rug

SIZE: About 2¾″ × 3¾″.

MATERIALS: *Pingouin Pingolaine* yarn, white and fuchsia. #2 knitting needles, or any needles which will give the stitch gauge below.

GAUGE: In SS, 8 sts = 1″; 8 rows = 1″.

DIRECTIONS: With white yarn, cast on 27 sts. Work 4 rows in SDS. Following chart, continue working 4 sts at beg and end of each row in SDS, while working pat in SS using fuchsia yarn. When pat is complete, work 4 rows in SDS. Cast off. Block to measurements.

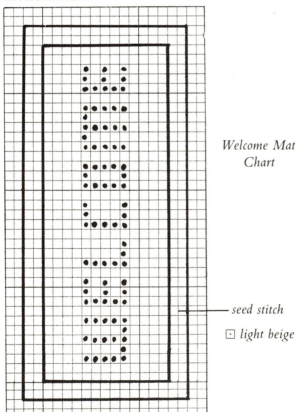

Welcome Mat Chart

— *seed stitch*

⊡ *light beige*

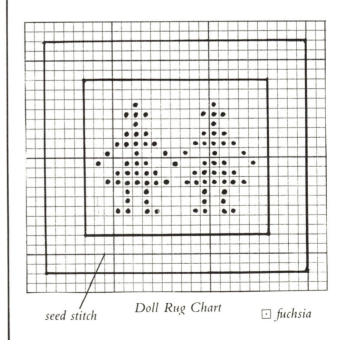

seed stitch   *Doll Rug Chart*   ⊡ *fuchsia*

Scatter Rug

SIZE: About 2½″ × 3½″.

MATERIALS: *Susan Bates® Softura™ Baby Yarn,* white. #2 knitting needles, or any needles which will give the stitch gauge below.

GAUGE: 7 sts = 1″.

DIRECTIONS: Cast on 26 sts. Work in pat as follows:

Row 1: K 2, P 2 across row.
Row 2: Rep Row 1.
Row 3: P 2, K 2 across row.
Row 4: Rep Row 3.

Work in pat until piece measures 2¼″. Cast off loosely in pat. Block to measurements.

Make 12 tassels, each ½″ long. Attach 6 tassels, evenly spaced, to each short side of rug.

Table or Sideboard Runner

SIZE: 1¼″ × 6½″ blocked.

MATERIALS: *Susan Bates® Fashion Tone™ Mercerized Cotton,* cream or desired color. #0 knitting needles, or any needles which will give the stitch gauge below.

GAUGE: In pat, 9 sts = 1¼″.

DIRECTIONS: Cast on 9 sts. Work in pat as follows:
Row 1: [Yo, P 2 tog] twice, (K, P, K, P, K) in next st, [yo, P 2 tog] twice.
Row 2: [Yo, P 2 tog] twice, K 5, [yo, P 2 tog] twice.
Row 3: Rep Row 2.
Row 4: Rep Row 2.
Row 5: [Yo, P 2 tog] twice, s1 1, K 1, psso, K 1, K 2 tog, [yo, P 2 tog] twice.
Row 6: [Yo, P 2 tog] twice, s1 1, K 2 tog, psso, [yo, P 2 tog] twice.

Rep these 6 rows until piece measures 6½″ or desired length. Cast off; weave in ends. Block to measurements.

Garter Stitch Rug and Pillow

SIZE: Rug, about 4″ × 6½″. Pillow, 1½″ square.

MATERIALS: *Bucilla® Fingering Yarn,* one skein each, scarlet and white. #0 knitting needles, or any needles which will give the stitch gauge below. Steel crochet hook, #3. Large-eyed needle. Stuffing for pillow.

GAUGE: 8 sts = 1″.

NOTE: See page 9 for crochet abbreviations.

DIRECTIONS: Rug: Make 6 squares as follows: With scarlet, cast 2 sts on #0 knitting needles. K 1 row. Knitting every row, inc 1 st at beg of each row to 17 sts. Attach white; continue to inc to 20 sts. Continuing in white, dec 1 st at beg of each row for next 3 rows; break off white. Attach scarlet; dec 1 st at beg of each row until 2 sts remain on needle. K 2 tog; cut yarn and pull through loop to finish.

Block each square to measure 1¾″ × 1¾″. Following diagram for placement, weave squares tog with matching yarn.

Crocheted Edging: With crochet hook #3 and scarlet, work 18 sc along short sides, 3 sc in corners, and 27 sc along long sides of rug. Make picots on both short edges as follows: ★ ch 3, 1 sc in second ch from hook, skip 1 st, 1 sc in next st. Repeat from ★ across. Fasten off. Block to measurements.

Pillow: With scarlet, cast 2 sts on #0 needles. K 1 row. Knitting every row, inc 1 st at beg of each row to 13 sts. Attach white; continue to inc to 15 sts. Continuing in white, dec 1 st at beg of each row for next 2 rows; break off white. Attach scarlet; dec 1 st at beg of each row until 2 sts remain on needle. K 2 tog; cut yarn and pull through loop to finish.

Rep for second side of pillow, reversing colors. With wrong sides facing, whip-stitch 3 sides of pillow pieces tog and stuff with cotton or fiberfill. Whip-stitch remaining edges tog.

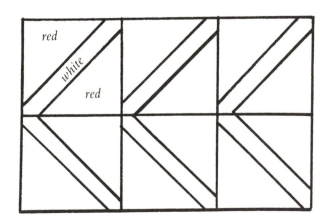

Garter Stitch Rug Diagram

White Pillow

SIZE: 1¼″ × 1½″, including edging.

MATERIALS: (*Belding*) *Lily® Pearl Cotton Mercerized Size 5,* white. #0 knitting needles, or any needles which will give the stitch gauge below. Steel crochet hook #3. Stuffing.

GAUGE: In SS, 4 sts = ½″; 6 rows = ½″.

NOTE: See page 9 for crochet abbreviations.

DIRECTIONS: Cast on 15 sts. Work 12 rows in SS; cast off on P row. Fold knitted piece in half crosswise; join with an sc in each st (*including folded edge*) using a #3 crochet hook; add stuffing before closing last side. Crochet edging as follows: ★ 2 dc in sc, ss in next sc. Repeat from ★ around. Fasten off.

A   B   C

Throw Pillows

SIZES: Each pillow is about ¾″ square.

MATERIALS: (*Belding*) *Lily® Pearl Cotton Mercerized Size 5, or Six Strand Floss,* blue, yellow, and orange. #1 knitting needles. Large-eyed needle. Stuffing.

DIRECTIONS: Blue Stockinette Stitch Pillow: (A) Cast on 8 sts. Work 16 rows in K 1 row, P 1 row. Cast off loosely. Fold knitted piece in half, right side out, matching short edges; whip-stitch 2 sides. Stuff pillow, then whip-stitch third side closed.

Yellow Seed Stitch Pillow: (B) Cast on 8 sts. Work in pat for 17 rows as follows:
Row 1: K 1, P 1 across row.
Row 2: P 1, K 1 across row.
Cast off loosely in pat. Finish as for blue pillow.

Orange Garter Stitch Pillow: (C) Cast on 8 sts. K 16 rows. Cast off loosely. Finish as for blue pillow.

Floor Pillow

SIZE: About 2½″ square.

MATERIALS: (*Belding*) *Lily® Pearl Cotton Mercerized Size 3,* red and maroon. #1 knitting needles, or any needles which will give the stitch gauge below. Large-eyed needle. Stuffing.

GAUGE: In pat, 9 sts = 1″; 10 rows = 1″.

DIRECTIONS: With red, cast on 20 sts. K across row (*wrong side of work*). Continue in corn-on-the-cob st as follows:

Row 1: (*Attach maroon.*) ★ K 1, sl 1. Rep from ★ across, K the last st.
Row 2 (*maroon*): ★ Sl 1 with yarn forward, K 1 with yarn back. Rep from ★ across (*sl all the light sts; K all the dark sts*).

Row 3: (*Attach red.*) ★ Sl 1, K 1 into back of st. Rep from ★ across (*K all the light sts; sl all the dark sts*).
Row 4 (*red*): ★ K 1 with yarn forward, sl 1 with yarn back. Rep from ★ across (*K all the light sts; sl all the dark sts*).

These 4 rows form the pat. Continue in pat until piece measures 2¼″. Break off maroon; work 2¼″ more in SS, using red. Cast off.

Finishing: Fold knitted piece in half, with *wrong* sides facing, matching short edges. Whip-stitch around 2 sides, fill pillow with stuffing, then whip-stitch third side closed.

Braid 3 strands of maroon to 9″ length. Slip-stitch around edges of pillow.

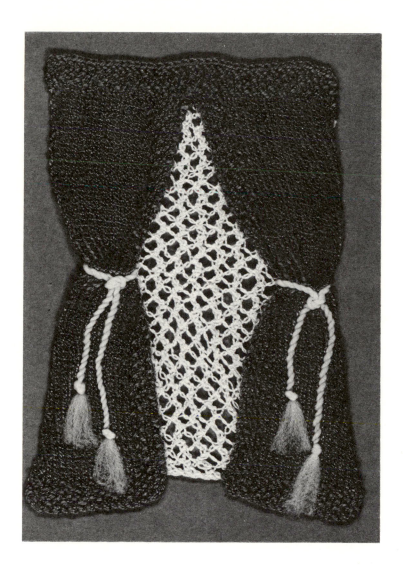

Tie-Back Curtains

SIZE: Each curtain, 2″ × 6½″ long.

MATERIALS: *DMC Pearl Cotton #5,* 2 skeins blue. #1 knitting needles, or any needles which will give the stitch gauge below. White cord for ties, two 10″ lengths. Stitch holder.

GAUGE: In SS, 9 sts = 1″; 12 rows = 1″.

DIRECTIONS: Cast on 19 sts. Work 4 rows in SDS. Working 4 sts at right edge of right side in SDS, continue working curtain in SS until work measures 6¼″; place sts on st holder.

Cast on 19 sts. Work second curtain in same manner as first, with SDS border along left edge. When second curtain is same length as the first, place first curtain back on needles with SDS borders at center. Work SDS across entire row (*38 sts*). Work 5 more rows in SDS. Cast off. Block to measurements.

Lace Curtain

SIZE: 4¼″ × 6½″.

MATERIALS: *DMC Pearl Cotton #8,* 1 ball white or desired color. #0 knitting needles or any needles which will give the stitch gauge below.

GAUGE: 27 sts = 4¼″; 16 rows = 1″.

DIRECTIONS: Cast on 27 sts. Work in pat as follows:
Row 1: P (*wrong side*).
Row 2: K 1, ★ yo, K 2 tog. Repeat from ★ to end.
Row 3: P.
Row 4: ★ Sl 1, K 1, psso, yo. Repeat from ★ to last st, end yo, K 1.

These 4 rows form the pat. Work in pat until piece measures 6½″ or desired length. Cast off loosely in P. Block to measurements.

Short Lace Curtain

SIZE: 3½″ × 3½″ blocked.

MATERIALS: *Phildar Perlé No 8*, white. #0 knitting needles, or any needles which will give the stitch gauge below.

GAUGE: In pat, 8 rows = 1″.

DIRECTIONS: Cast on 33 sts. Work 2 rows in GS, then work in pat as follows:
Row 1: K 2, K 1, yo, K 1, ★ P 1, K 1, yo, K 1. Rep from ★ to last 2 sts, K 2.
Row 2: K 2, P 3, ★ K 1, P 3. Rep from ★ to last 2 sts, K 2.
Row 3: K 2, sl 1, K 2, psso, ★ P 1, sl 1 with yarn in back, K 2, psso. Rep from ★ to last 2 sts, K 2.
Row 4: K 2, P 2, ★ K 1, P 2. Rep from ★ to last 2 sts, K 2.

Rep Rows 1–4 until piece measures 3⅜″. Work 2 rows in GS. Cast off loosely in K. Block to measurements.

Double Drapes

SIZE: 4″ long × 3″ wide (blocked pair).

MATERIALS: For each pair of drapes, 2 skeins *Susan Bates Anchor® Stranded Cotton*, crimson. #0 knitting needles, or any needles which will give the stitch gauge below.

GAUGE: 8 sts = 1″; 8 rows = 1″.

DIRECTIONS: With full 6 strands of floss, cast 18 sts on #0 needles. Work in pat as follows:
Row 1 (*wrong side*): P.
Row 2: K 2, ★ yo, K 2 tog, K 2, sl 1, K 1, psso, yo, K 2. Rep from ★ to end.

Rep these 2 rows until piece measures 3″. Cast off loosely. Make second drape in same manner. Block each drape to 2″ × 3″ size. With right sides facing up, attach top inner corners of drapes tog. Repeat for as many drapes as needed to cover windows.

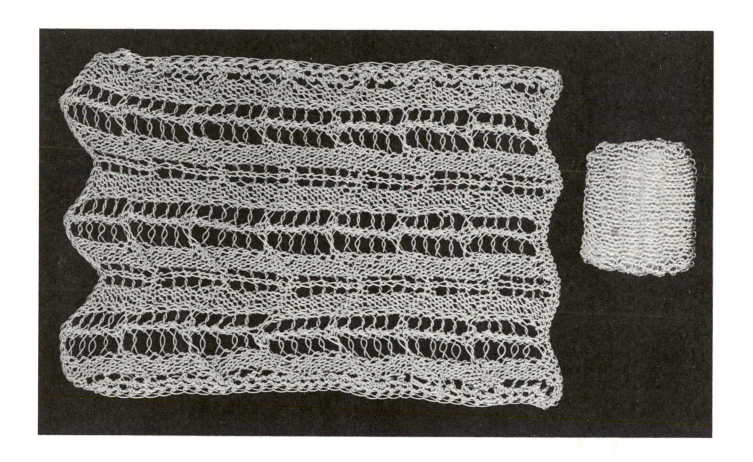

Scallop Pattern Bedspread and Pillow

SIZES: Bedspread, about 4½″ × 7½″. Pillow, about 1¾″ × 2″.

MATERIALS: (*Belding Lily*) *Daisy Mercrochet Size 30*, ecru. #1 knitting needles, or any needles which will give the stitch gauge below. Steel crochet hook #3. Large-eyed needle and stuffing for pillow.

NOTE: See page 9 for crochet abbreviations.

DIRECTIONS: Bedspread: Gauge: In pat, 14 sts = 1½″; 12 rows = 1″.
Cast on 43 sts. Work in pat as follows:
Row 1: (*wrong side*) P.
Row 2: K 1, ★ yo, K 3, ssk, yo, sl 1, K 1, psso, yo, K 2 tog, K 3, yo, K 1. Rep from ★ to end of row.
Row 3: P.
Row 4: Rep Row 2.
Row 5: P.
Row 6: Rep Row 2.
Row 7: P.
Row 8: Rep Row 2.
Row 9: P.

Row 10: Rep Row 2.
Row 11: K.
Row 12: P.

These 12 rows form the pat. Work in pat until piece measures 7½″ (*7 complete pats*). Cast off loosely. Block to measurements. With crochet hook #3 and cotton, make about 36 sc along one long edge of bedspread. Ch 1, turn, work sc into each sc, fasten off. Repeat on opposite side. Press flat.

Pillow: Gauge: 14 rows = 1″; 8 sts = 1″.
Cast on 18 sts. Work in pat as follows:
Row 1: K.
Row 2: P.
Row 3: K.
Row 4: K.

These 4 rows form the pat; Row 4 forms the ridge. Rep until 11 ridges are made. Cast off loosely. Block to measurements. Fold knitted piece in half, ridged side out, matching short edges; whip-stitch 2 sides. Stuff pillow, then whip-stitch third side closed.

Garter Stitch Afghan

SIZE: 5½" × 6½", blocked, excluding tassels.

MATERIALS: *DMC Pearl Cotton #8,* blue ombre. #1 knitting needles, or any needles which will give the stitch gauge below.

GAUGE: 8 sts = 1"; 8 rows = 1".

DIRECTIONS: Cast on 50 sts. Work in GS until piece measures 5½" or desired width. Cast off loosely. Block to measurements.

Make 52 tassels, each ¼" long. Attach, evenly spaced, to 2 long edges and 1 short edge of afghan.

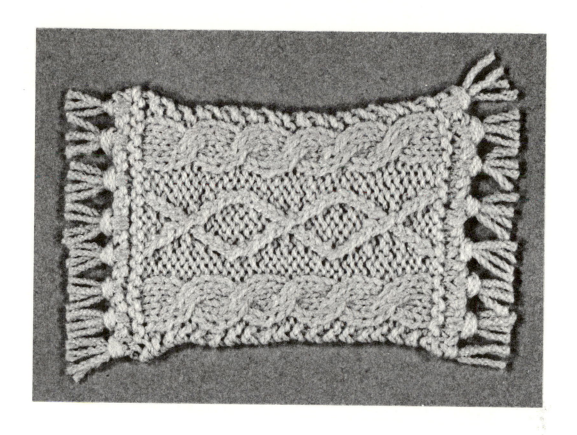

Aran Knit Afghan

SIZE: 2½″ × 4¼″, blocked.

MATERIALS: *Coats & Clark Red Heart "Wintuk" Baby Yarn,* eggshell. #3 knitting needles, or any needles which will give the stitch gauge below. #3 dp needle.

GAUGE: 22 sts = 2½″; 11 rows = 1″.

DIRECTIONS: Cast on 22 sts. K 2 rows. Work in pat as follows:

Row 1: K 1, P 1, K 4, P 2, K 1, P 4, K 1, P 2, K 4, P 1, K 1.

Row 2: K 2, P 4, K 2, P 1, K 4, P 1, K 2, P 4, K 2.

Row 3: K 1, P 1, K 4, P 2, CF 1, P 2, CB 1, P 2, K 4, P 1, K 1.

Row 4: K 2, P 4, K 3, P 1, K 2, P 1, K 3, P 4, K 2.

Row 5: K 1, P 1, K 4, P 3, CF 1, CB 1, P 3, K 4, P 1, K 1.

Row 6: K 2, P 4, K 4, P 2, K 4, P 4, K 2.

Row 7: K 1, P 1, CF 2, P 4, [K into back of second st then into front of first st on left needle, slip both sts off tog] once, P 4, CF 2, P 1, K 1.

Row 8: Rep Row 6.

Row 9: K 1, P 1, K 4, P 3, CB 1, CF 1, P 3, K 4, P 1, K 1.

Row 10: Rep Row 4.

Row 11: K 1, P 1, K 4, P 2, CB 1, P 2, CF 1, P 2, K 4, P 1, K 1.

Row 12: Rep Row 2.

Row 13: K 1, P 1, CF 2, P 2, CF 1, P 2, CB 1, P 2, CF 2, P 1, K 1.

Row 14: Rep Row 4.

Row 15: Rep Row 5. Continue to follow pattern in numerical sequence between Rows 2–15 until piece measures 4″ (*2 full diamonds, 2 half diamonds*). End with Row 1 instead of Row 13 for second half diamond. K 2 rows. Cast off. Block to measurements.

Make 16 tassels, each ¼″ long. Attach 8, evenly spaced to each short end of afghan.

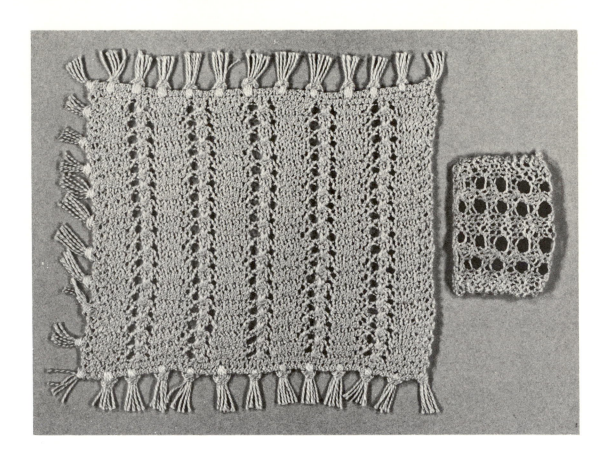

Lacy Bedspread and Pillow

SIZES: Bedspread, 5″ × 6¼″ without fringe. Pillow, 2½″ × 1¾″.

MATERIALS: *Coats and Clark's Pearl Cotton Size 5,* 3 balls yellow. #0 and #1 knitting needles, or any needles which will give the stitch gauges below. **For Pillow:** Small stuffed pillow, about 2½″ × 1¾″. Large-eyed needle.

DIRECTIONS: Bedspread: Gauge: Working in pat with #0 needles, 8 sts = 1″; 12 rows = 1″. Cast 47 sts on #0 needles. Work 2 rows in GS. Continue in pat as follows:
Row 1: K.
Row 2: K 2, P to last 2 sts, K 2.
Row 3: K 2, ★ P 4, yo, sl 1, P 2 tog, psso, yo, P 1. Rep from ★ to last 5 sts, P 3, K 2.
Row 4: K 2, ★ K 4, P 3, K 1. Rep from ★ to last 5 sts, K 5.

These 4 rows form the pat. Continue in pat until piece measures 4¾″. Work 3 rows in GS. Cast off loosely. Block to measurements.

Make 35 tassels, each ½″ long. Attach, evenly spaced, to 2 long edges and 1 short edge of afghan.

Pillow: Gauge: Working in GS on #1 needles, 8 sts = 1″; 8 rows = 1″.
Cast 16 sts on #1 needles. Work in pat as follows:
Row 1: K.
Row 2: K 2, P 12, K 2.
Row 3: K 2, P 2, yo, sl 1, P 2 tog, psso, yo, P 3, yo, sl 1, P 2 tog, psso, yo, P 1, K 2.
Row 4: K 3, P 3, K 3, P 3, K 4.

These 4 rows form the pat. Continue in pat until 5 rows of holes are formed, then change to GS and work straight for 1¾″ (or long enough to match the pat side). Cast off. Block to measurements.

Fold knitted piece in half with wrong sides facing, matching 2½″ edges. Whip-stitch short sides tog, insert pillow, and whip-stitch third side closed.

Floral Bedroom Set

SIZES: See individual directions.

MATERIALS: *J. & P. Coats "Knit-Cro-Sheen,"* 1 ball ecru for all items, #0 knitting needles, or any size needles which will give the stitch gauge below. Steel crochet hook #3.

GAUGE: In GS, 8 sts = 1"; 8 rows = 1".

NOTE: See page 9 for crochet abbreviations.

DIRECTIONS: Bedspread (*5¼" × 6¾" without edging*): Cast on 56 sts; work in pat as follows:
Row 1: K.
Row 2: K.
Row 3: K 6, ★ K 2 tog, yo twice, K 2 tog, K 16.

Rep from ★ across, ending K 2 tog, yo twice, K 2 tog, K 6.
Row 4: K 8, P 1, ★ K 19, P 1. Rep from ★ across, ending P 1, K 7.
Row 5: K 4, ★ [K 2 tog, yo twice, K 2 tog] twice, K 12. Rep from ★ across, ending [K 2 tog, yo twice, K 2 tog] twice, K 4.
Row 6: K 6, P 1, K 3, P 1, ★ K 15, P 1, K 3, P 1. Rep from ★ across, ending K 5.
Row 7: Rep Row 3.
Row 8: Rep Row 4.
Row 9: Rep Row 5.
Row 10: Rep Row 6.
Row 11: Rep Row 3.
Row 12: Rep Row 4.
Row 13: K.

Row 14: K.
Row 15: ★ K 16, K 2 tog, yo twice, K 2 tog. Rep from ★ across, ending K 2 tog, yo twice, K 2 tog, K 16.
Row 16: K 18, P 1, ★ K 19, P 1. Rep from ★ across, ending K 17.
Row 17: K 14, ★ [K 2 tog, yo twice, K 2 tog] twice, K 12. Rep from ★ across, ending K 14.
Row 18: K 16, P 1, K 3, P 1, ★ K 15, P 1, K 3, P 1. Rep from ★ across, ending K 15.
Row 19: Rep Row 15.
Row 20: Rep Row 16.
Row 21: Rep Row 17.
Row 22: Rep Row 18.
Row 23: Rep Row 15.
Row 24: Rep Row 16.

Rep Rows 1–24 twice more (*3 times in all*). Then work Rows 1–14 once. Cast off. Block to measurements.

To make crochet edging, attach yarn to corner, beginning at one long edge with right side facing. ★ Ch 7, sc into fourth st. Repeat from ★ across (*14 lps made*). Work 1 lp on corner, 10 lps along short edge, 1 lp on corner, and 14 lps on long edge. Turn. On next row, ★ ch 7, sc in each ch 7 lp; work from ★ along all 3 sides, working 1 lp in corner at end of row. Turn. For outer row, ss to fourth ch of previous row, ★ ch 7, sc in each ch 7 lp; work from ★ along all 3 sides. Fasten off. Press lightly if necessary.

Drapes (*4″ wide × 5¼″ long for double drapes*): Cast on 18 sts; work in pat as follows:
Rows 1–4: K.
Row 5: K 7, K 2 tog, yo twice, K 2 tog, K 7.
Row 6: K 9, P 1, K 8.
Row 7: K 5, [K 2 tog, yo twice, K 2 tog] twice, K 5.
Row 8: K 7, P 1, K 3, P 1, K 6.
Row 9: Rep Row 5.
Row 10: Rep Row 6.
Row 11: Rep Row 7.
Row 12: Rep Row 8.
Row 13: Rep Row 5.
Row 14: Rep Row 6.
Rows 15–18: K.

Work Rows 1–18 three more times or to desired length. Cast off. Make second drape in same manner.

Make crocheted valence as follows: Using #3 crochet hook, ch 33. Sc in third ch from hook, sc in each ch across. Turn.
Row 1: Ch 7, skip 2 sc, sc in next sc. Work to end of row in same manner. Turn.
Row 2: Ss to center of first ch 7 lp, ch 7, sc into each ch 7 lp. Turn.
Row 3: Rep Row 2. Fasten off.

With right sides up, attach inside edge of 2 drapes tog, making 1 double drape. Slip-stitch valence to top right side of drapes. Rep for as many windows as needed.

Pillow (*1½″ square without edging*): Additional Materials: 2 pieces desired color felt, each 1½″ square. Stuffing. Needle and matching thread.
Cast on 10 sts; work in pat as follows:
Row 1: K.
Row 2: K.
Row 3: K 3, K 2 tog, yo twice, K 2 tog, K 3.
Row 4: K 5, P 1, K 4.
Row 5: K 1, [K 2 tog, yo twice, K 2 tog] twice, K 1.
Row 6: K 3, P 1, K 3, P 1, K 2.
Row 7: Rep Row 3.
Row 8: Rep Row 4.
Row 9: Rep Row 5.
Row 10: Rep Row 6.
Row 11: Rep Row 3.
Row 12: Rep Row 4.
Row 13: K.
Row 14: K.
Rows 15–22: K.

Cast off. Slip-stitch 2 pieces of felt tog on 3 sides; stuff, then sew fourth side closed. Fold knitted piece in half with wrong sides facing, matching short edges. Using a #3 crochet hook and sc's, join knitted pieces tog on 2 sides. Insert felt pillow, sc third side closed. Ch 4, skip 1 sc, sc in next sc; continue all around, joining at end with ss. Fasten off.

Rug (*3½″ diameter without edging*): Additional Materials: DMC Pearl Cotton #3, 1 skein to match felt for pillow. #2 knitting needles. #2 steel crochet hook. Using a double strand of *Knit-Cro-Sheen* and #2 needles, cast on 10 sts. Work Rows 1–14 for pillow. Cast off.

With pearl cotton and #2 crochet hook, sc around knitted square.
Rnd 2: Sc in each sc, making 2 sc in each third sc.
Rnd 3: Rep Rnd 2.
Rnd 4: Sc in each sc, working 2 sc in each fourth sc around.
Rnd 5: Sc in each sc, working 2 sc in each fifth sc around.
Rnd 6: Sc in each sc around.

Attach 1 strand of *Knit-Cro-Sheen* and work as follows:
Rnd 1: Ch 7, skip 2 sc, sc in next sc, all around.
Rnd 2: Ss to center of first ch 7 lp, ch 7, sc in next ch 7 lp, all around. Join at end with ss. Fasten off.

Canopy Bed Set

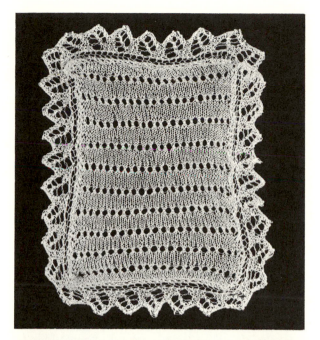

SIZE: Bedspread, 6" × 8", blocked. Canopy, 8½" × 9½", including edging.

MATERIALS: *Phildar Perlé No. 8,* white. #0 knitting needles, or any needles which will give the stitch gauge below.

GAUGE: In SS, 7 sts = 1"; 7 rows = ½".

DIRECTIONS: Bedspread: Cast on 44 sts. Work 4 rows in SS, then work in pat as follows:
Row 1: K.
Row 2: K.
Row 3: P 1, ★ yo, P 2 tog. Rep from ★ across, ending P 1.
Row 4: K.
Row 5: K.
Row 6: P.
Row 7: K.
Row 8: P.
Row 9: K.
Row 10: P.
Row 11: K.
Row 12: K.
Row 13: P 2, ★ yo, P 2 tog. Rep from ★ across.
Row 14: K.
Row 15: K.
Row 16: P.
Row 17: K.
Row 18: P.
Row 19: K.
Row 20: P.

Work these 20 rows of pat until 8 eyelet rows have been completed, then work rows 1–18 (*10 eyelets*). Cast off very loosely in K.

Picot Edging: ★ Make a loop in the yarn, put this loop on left needle, and cast 2 more sts on left needle, making 3 sts in all (*Figure 1*). K and cast off 2 of the 3 sts, leaving 1 st on needle (*Figure 2*). Transfer remaining st to left needle and rep from ★. Make 85 picots or enough to fit around all 4 sides of bedspread. Cast off. Chain should resemble picot point chain diagram (*Figure 3*).

Carefully block bedspread to measurements, then sew picot edging around bedspread.

Canopy: Work same as for bedspread up to picot edging, then work lace edging as follows: With white, cast on 10 sts.
Row 1: Sl 1, K 2, yo, K 2 tog, [yo twice, K 2 tog] twice, K 1.
Row 2: K 3, [P 1, K 1] twice, yo, K 2 tog, K 3.

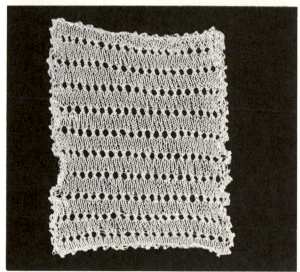

Row 3: Sl 1, K 2, yo, K 2 tog, K 2, [yo twice, K 2 tog] twice, K 1.
Row 4: K 3, P 1, K 2, P 1, K 4, yo, K 2 tog, K 1.
Row 5: Sl 1, K 2, yo, K 2 tog, K 4, [yo twice, K 2 tog] twice, K 1.
Row 6: K 3, P 1, K 2, P 1, K 6, yo, K 2 tog, K 1.
Row 7: Sl 1, K 2, yo, K 2 tog, K 11.
Row 8: Cast off 6 sts, K 6, yo, K 2 tog, K 1.

These 8 rows form the pat. Continue working in pat until 33 points are made, or you have made enough lace to fit around canopy. Cast off. Carefully block canopy to measurements, then sew lace edging around canopy.

———— *Picot Point Chain Diagram* ————

Figure 1 ⌐*Figure 2* *Figure 3*

Acu pressure.   5 points.   L.

1. <u>On the Top of your elbow</u> — (Digestive system)
    Hold the elbow with 4 fingers and press with
    your thumb — This is a pumping action. —
    Press and let go.

2. <u>Below the knee</u>   — (Circulation.)
    Feel the bone Measure 4 fingers down and
    1 thumb To left or outside of leg

3. <u>Inside of ankle.</u>   — (Bloatedness(
    Go for prominance of bone. 4 fingers up shin
    bone. Support with 4 fingers and press.

4. <u>Between 2 Toes.</u>   —   (liver & circulation)
    Measure 2 Thumbs away from where the
    skin is.

5. <u>Back of Neck.</u>   —   (Immune system + posture.)
    Run your finger down back of neck, Find Spinal
    Cord. Press between 1st & 2nd Vertibrae.

    <u>Extra Point on Hand.</u> —   Headaches.
    Stretch thumb & Index finger and press skin
    between

Switchable Yarns

The yarns within each separate category in this listing are interchangeable, which means that a similar appearance and gauge will result if one yarn is substituted for another. The yarns in each category are listed alphabetically by manufacturer; the following manufacturers are represented:

Susan Bates	DMC
Belding Lily	Laines Anny Blatt
Bernat	Paternayan
Brunswick	Phildar
Bucilla	Pingouin
Coats & Clark's	Plymouth
Conshohocken	Tahki

All the yarns within each category have a similar texture, thus much the same results can be achieved by using any one of them. Some yarns within a category may differ slightly in weight from others within the same category; however the differences are so slight that a similar gauge will result if the hook or needles are changed one size larger or smaller. It is essential to test your gauge when making a substitution by crocheting or knitting a swatch before beginning a project.

Six Strand Floss

MANUFACTURER/NAME	FIBER	WEIGHT/YARDAGE
Susan Bates Anchor® Stranded Cotton	cotton	8.7 yds
(Belding) Lily® Six Strand Floss	cotton	2 oz tubes
J. & P. Coats Deluxe Six Strand Floss	cotton	9 yds
DMC Six Strand Embroidery Floss	cotton	8.7 yds

Pearl Cotton

MANUFACTURER/NAME	FIBER	WEIGHT/YARDAGE
Pearl Cotton No. 3		
(Belding) Lily® Pearl Cotton Mercerized Size 3	cotton	2 oz tube
Bernat® Cassino® (2 strands)	cotton	1¾ oz ball
DMC Pearl Cotton #3	cotton	16.4 yd skein
Pearl Cotton No. 5		
(Belding) Lily® Pearl Cotton Mercerized Size 5	cotton	2 oz tube
Bernat® Cassino® (1 strand)	cotton	1¾ oz ball
Coats & Clark's Pearl Cotton Size 5	cotton	50 yd ball
DMC Pearl Cotton #5	cotton	27.3 yd skein, 53 yd ball
Phildar Perlé No. 5	cotton	1 oz ball
Pearl Cotton No. 8		
(Belding) Lily's Sil-Tone	cotton	75 yd ball
DMC Pearl Cotton #8	cotton	95 yd ball
Phildar Perlé No. 8	cotton	1 oz ball

Knit, Crochet, and Tatting Yarns

MANUFACTURER/NAME	FIBER	WEIGHT/YARDAGE
Lightweight		
(Belding) Lily Tatting Crochet	cotton	125 & 400 yds
(Belding Lily) Daisy Mercerized Crochet Cotton No. 30	cotton	500 yd skein
(Belding Lily) Daisy Mercrochet Size 30	cotton	300 & 500 yd balls
Coats & Clark's Tatting Crochet Size 70	cotton	125 yds
Clark's Big Ball #30	cotton	550 yds
J. & P. Coats Six Cord Mercerized #30	cotton	350 yds
DMC Cébélia Size 30	cotton	563 yds
DMC Cordonnet Spécial #50	cotton	286 yds
DMC Cordonnet Spécial #40	cotton	249 yds
DMC Cordonnet Spécial #30	cotton	216 yds
DMC Fil A Dentelles	cotton	106 yds
Medium-Weight		
Susan Bates® Fashion-Tone™ Mercerized Cotton	cotton	300 yds
(Belding Lily) Big Deal	cotton	450 yds
(Belding) Lily 100% Polyester	polyester	500 yds
(Belding) Lily 18th Century Mercerized Crochet & Bedspread Cotton	cotton	500 yds
(Belding) Lily Frost-Tone	cotton	600 yds
(Belding) Lily® "Glo-Tone" Mercerized Cotton	cotton	175 yds
(Belding) Lily® Sky-Tone	cotton	300 yds
J. & P. Coats "Knit-Cro-Sheen"	cotton	175 yds
DMC Cébélia Size 20	cotton	405 yds
DMC Cébélia Size 10	cotton	282 yds
DMC Cordonnet Spécial #20	cotton	174 yds
DMC Cordonnet Spécial #10	cotton	124 yds
Phildar Relais No 8	cotton	410 yds
Heavy-Weight		
(Belding) Lily Soft Spun Yarn	cotton	150 yds
(Belding) Lily® Antique Crochet/Knitting Tricot	cotton	500 yds
(Belding) Lily® Double Quick Mercerized Crochet Cotton	cotton	115 yds
Bucilla® Wondersheen	cotton	400 yds
Conshohocken Softball™ Featherweight	cotton	354 yds
DMC Brilliant Crochet Cotton®	cotton	218 yds
Pingouin cordonnet	100% acrylic	120 yds
Pingouin fil d'écosse No. 5	cotton	175 yds

Persian Yarns

MANUFACTURER/NAME	FIBER	WEIGHT/YARDAGE
Bernat 1-2-3 Ply® Persian-Type Yarn	100% acrylic	12½ yd skein
Brunswick Brunsana® Persian Yarn	100% virgin wool	8.8 yd & 40 yd skeins
Bucilla® Persian Needlepoint and Crewel Wool	100% virgin wool	40 yd skein
Coats & Clark Red Heart Persian Type Needlepoint & Crewel Yarn	100% acrylic	12 yd skein
DMC Laine Divisible Floralia®—3 Ply Persian Wool	100% wool	5.4 yd & 27.3 yd skeins
Paternayan Paterna Persian Yarn	100% virgin wool	8 yd skein
Plymouth Persian Needlepoint Yarn	100% virgin wool	1 lb reelings or cones

Baby and Fingering Yarns

MANUFACTURER/NAME	FIBER	WEIGHT/YARDAGE
Susan Bates® Softura™ Baby Yarn	100% orlon acrylic	1.76 oz
Bernat® Berella® 3-Ply Fingering	60% acrylic/40% nylon	1 oz
Brunswick Fairhaven® 3 Ply Fingering Yarn	100% wool	1 oz
Brunswick Windspun® Sock & Fingering Yarn	100% orlon	1 oz
Bucilla® Fingering Yarn	100% orlon acrylic	1 oz
Coats & Clark Red Heart Cashelle™ Baby Yarn	100% orlon acrylic	1.76 oz
Coats & Clark Red Heart "Wintuk" Baby Yarn	100% orlon acrylic	2 oz
Laines Anny Blatt 'Lady Blatt'	100% wool	315 yds
Phildar Loisirs	85% acrylic/15% wool	1¾ oz
Phildar Luxe	85% acrylic/15% wool	1¾ oz
Pingouin Mademoiselle	100% acrylic	230 yds
Pingouin Pingolaine	100% pure new wool	220 yds
Pingouin Pingorex Baby	100% acrylic	265 yds
Tahki "Daphné"	60% wool/40% silk	125 yds

Mog had a medal.
She also had an egg every day for breakfast.
Mr and Mrs Thomas told all their friends about her.
They said, "Mog is really remarkable."
And they never – (or almost never) –
said, "Bother that cat!"

I've seen watch-dogs,
but never a watch-cat.
She will get a medal."
Debbie said, "I think she'd rather have an egg."

A policeman came and
they told him what had happened.
The policeman looked at Mog.
He said, "What a remarkable cat.

She meowed her biggest meow,
very sudden and very, very loud.
The man was surprised.
He dropped his bag.
It made a big noise
and everyone in the house woke up.

Mr Thomas ran down to the kitchen
and shouted, "A burglar!"
The burglar said, "Bother that cat!"
Mrs Thomas telephoned the police.
Debbie let Mog in
and Nicky hugged her.

Then she noticed something.
The house was not quite dark.
There was a little light moving about.
She looked through the window
and saw a man in the kitchen.
Mog thought, "Perhaps that man will let me in.
Perhaps he will give me my supper."

Mog ran out of the room
and right through the house
and out of her cat flap.
She was very sad.
The garden was dark.
The house was dark too.
Mog sat in the dark
and thought dark thoughts.
She thought, "Nobody likes me.
They've all gone to bed.
There's no one to let me in.
And they haven't even given me my supper."

Debbie shouted. Mog jumped.
Mr and Mrs Thomas said,
"Bother, bother, BOTHER that cat!"
Debbie said nothing.
She was still crying because of the bad dream.

The tiger wanted
to eat Debbie.
It was licking her hair.

Debbie had a dream.
It was a bad dream.
It was a dream about a tiger.

Mog thought, "Nobody likes me."
Then she thought, "Debbie likes me."
Debbie's door was open.
Debbie's bed was warm.
Debbie's hair was soft, like kitten fur.
Mog forgot that Debbie was not a kitten.

Mog had a rest too,
but Mr Thomas wanted to see the fight.
Mr Thomas said, "Bother that cat!"

Mrs Thomas said, "Bother that cat!"
Debbie said, "I think you look nicer without a hat."

Debbie gave Mog her supper
and Mog ate it all up.
Then Debbie and Nicky went to bed.

She could fly everywhere.
She could fly faster than the birds,
even quite big birds . . .
Suddenly she woke up.

Mog was very sleepy.
She found a nice warm, soft place
and went to sleep.
She had a lovely dream.
Mog dreamed that she had wings.

Mog ran right round the house.
And the dog ran after her.
She climbed over the fence.
She ran through the garden
and jumped up outside the kitchen window.
She meowed a big meow,
very sudden and very loud.

Mrs Thomas said, "Bother that cat!"
Debbie said, "It wasn't her fault."

The sun was not shining in the street after all.
It was raining.
A big dog came down the street.
Mog ran.
The dog ran too.

Mog looked through her cat flap.
It was raining in the garden.
Mog thought, "Perhaps the sun is shining in the street."
When the milkman came she ran out.
The milkman shut the door.

She ate an egg for her breakfast.
Mrs Thomas said, "Bother that cat!"
Debbie said, "Nicky doesn't like eggs anyway."

Then it was breakfast time.
Mog forgot that cats have milk for breakfast.
She forgot that cats only have eggs as a treat.

Once Mog had a very bad day.
Even the start of the day was bad.
Mog was still asleep.
Then Nicky picked her up.
He hugged her
and said, "Nice kitty!"
Mog said nothing.
But she was not happy.

Afterwards you could always tell
where she had sat.
This made Mr Thomas very sad.
He said, "Bother that cat!"
But Debbie said, "She's nice!"

In the end she sat outside the kitchen window
and meowed until someone let her in.

The garden always made Mog very excited.
She smelled all the smells.
She chased the birds.
She climbed the trees.
She ran round and round
with a big fluffed-up tail.
And then she forgot the cat flap.
She forgot that she had a cat flap.
She wanted to go back into the house,
but she couldn't remember how.

But most of all she forgot her cat flap.
The cat flap led from the kitchen
into the garden.
Mog could go out . . .

. . . and in
again.
It was
her
own
little
door.

Sometimes she ate her supper.
Then she forgot that she'd eaten it.

Sometimes she thought of something
in the middle of washing her leg.
Then she forgot to wash the rest of it.

Once she forgot
that cats can't fly.

Mr Thomas

Mrs Thomas

Nicky

Debbie

Once there was a cat called Mog and
she lived with a family called Thomas.
Mog was nice but not very clever.
She didn't understand a lot of things.
A lot of other things she forgot.
She was a very forgetful cat.

Mog

Mog
the
forgetful
cat

For our own Mog

Mog the Forgetful Cat is ideal
for children beginning to read as
it uses a limited vocabulary.

First published in hardback in Great Britain by
William Collins Sons & Co Ltd in 1970
20 19
First published in Great Britain in Picture Lions in 1975
New edition first published in 1993
15 17 19 20 18 16 14
Picture Lions is an imprint of the Children's Division,
part of HarperCollins Publishers Limited,
77-85 Fulham Palace Road, Hammersmith,
London W6 8JB

ISBN: 0 00 195507-1 (hardback)
ISBN: 0 00 664062-1 (Picture Lions)

The HarperCollins website address is
www.fireandwater.com

Printed in Hong Kong by Imago

the forgetful cat

Written and
illustrated by

Judith Kerr

PictureLions
An Imprint of HarperCollins*Publishers*

He scratched

and he twitched and he wriggled,

but it only made the scratchy, twitchy, itchy tickling worse!

He gathered up the Rhinoceros's skin and took it to his camp, where he filled it with as many dry, stale, tickly cake crumbs, and burned, sticky currants as he could possibly find...

Then, he dragged the skin back to the water's edge and climbed to the top of the nearest palm tree, where he waited for the Rhinoceros to come out of the water and put it back on.

The Rhinoceros did, of course. He buttoned it up beneath his tummy as he had always done before, and it tickled and prickled like toast crumbs in bed.

The Parsee spotted the skin on the shore. He smiled
the broadest of smiles and jigged the merriest jig as he
planned his *cleverest plan*...

Flinging his skin down on the sand, the Rhinoceros waddled straight in to the water, and blew *bubbles* out of his nose.

It was a very hot day; the sun beat down on the baking sand and the sky was a cloudless blue.

The Rhinoceros waddled down to the water's edge and took off his skin to bathe (for in those days it buttoned under his tummy).

He saw the Parsee, but did not mention the cake because he had eaten it all, and he had no manners.

He still doesn't have any manners now, and never will have any, I don't expect.

When the coast was clear, the Parsee climbed down from his perch, muttering to himself all the while:

"Them that takes cakes
Which the Parsee-man bakes
Makes themselves dreadful mistakes!"

If only the Rhinoceros had heard the Parsee's rhyme, things might have turned out differently.

Luckily for our story (but unluckily for the Rhinoceros), he did not hear the Parsee's warning, and, just five weeks later, he learned his lesson...

The Parsee took fright, and, leaving his cake, climbed to the top of the nearest palm tree.

He watched in terror as the Rhinoceros spiked the cake on the end of his horn and gobbled it all up!

Then, burping very rudely, he galumphed away across the sand.

Just as he was about to cut himself a slice to taste, the Parsee spotted a Rhinoceros waddling down from the beach.

He had a horn on his nose, two piggy little eyes, and very few manners.

In those days – for this was very long ago – the Rhinoceros's skin fitted him very tightly and he had no wrinkles at all.

Once upon a time, on a deserted island on the shores of the Red Sea, there lived a Parsee who was very fond of baking.

One day, he took flour, and water, and currants, and plums, and sugar, and things, and made himself an enormous cake, which was two feet across and over three feet high!

It was, of course, a Superior Comestible (that's Magic), and he put it on the stove and baked it and baked it until it was golden brown and smelled truly scrumptious.

How the
RHINO
got his SKIN

Retold from the Rudyard Kipling original
Illustrated by Ela Jarzabek

This story tells us how the rhino got his skin. In days past, the rhino's skin fit him tightly, with no wrinkles. One hot day, the rhino took off his skin to cool down. While his skin was off the Parsee man, whose cake he had stolen, took revenge on him. He rubbed cake-crumbs inside the rhino's skin, so that when the rhino wore his skin again, he itched and itched until he had big folds in his skin.

Rudyard Kipling, born in 1865 in what was then Bombay, India, grew up in love with everything about the country of India: the culture, the people, and the language. He began writing short stories inspired by his time in India, and in 1894 published his famous novel, *The Jungle Book*. The *Just So* stories began as Kipling's bedtime stories for his daughter Effie, and explain the various fantastic and strange ways animals came to look how they do today.

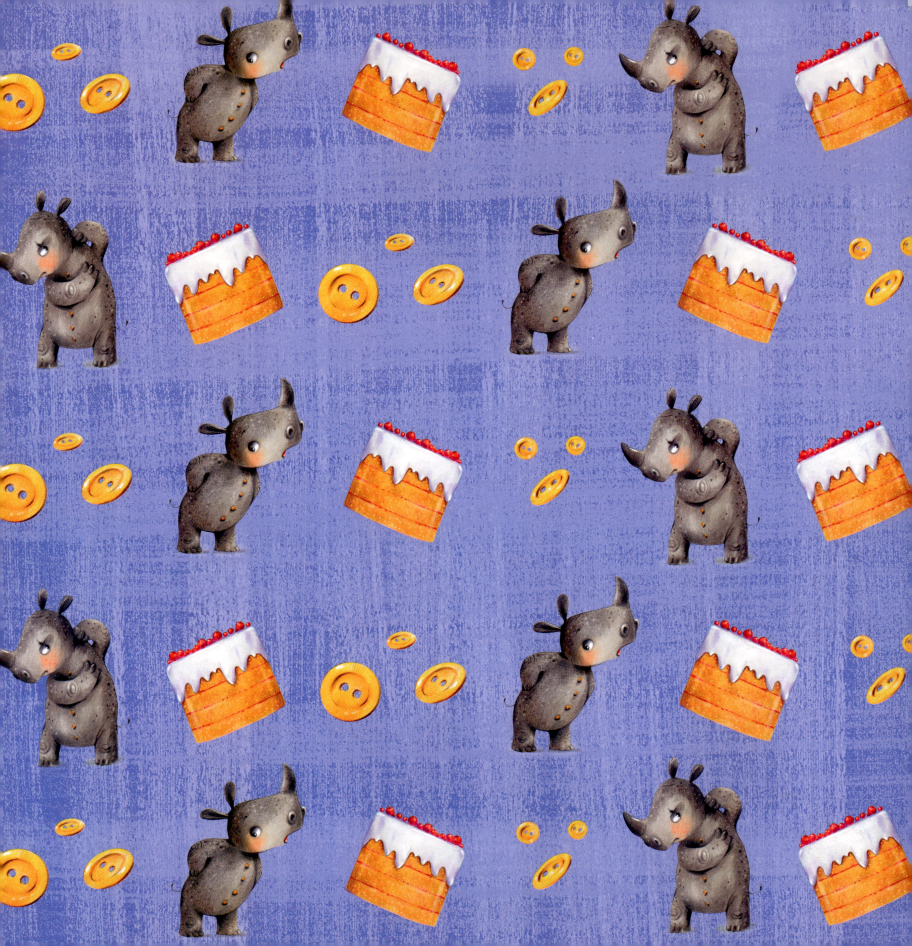

This Just So story belongs to:

_____

_____

Your name goes here!

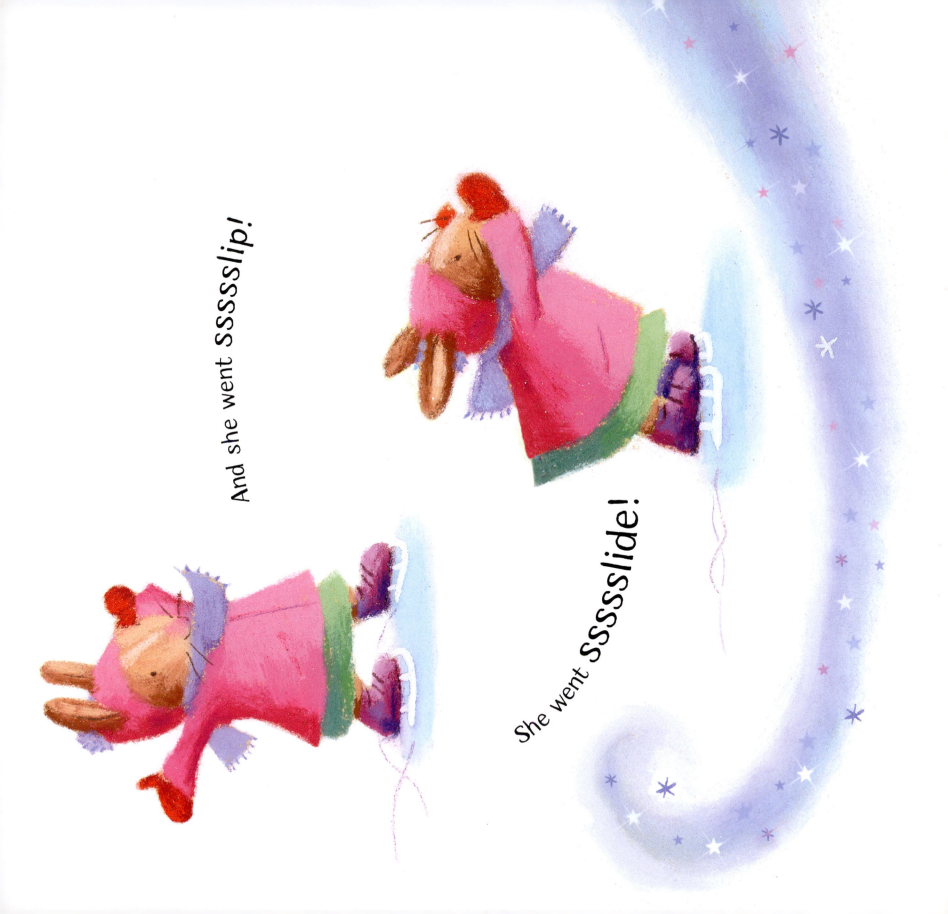

And she went SSSSSlip!

She went SSSSSlide!

So she laced up her boots,

and one paw . . .

two paws . . . .

she stepped on to the ice!

That made Bella feel a lot
more sure of herself.
"Maybe I can be a
skater too!" she said.

So Bella just sat and watched with Daddy.

Then she said. "Look at that funny bunny! I was a funny bunny when I made my snow-mouse, wasn't I?"

"Yes, you were!" laughed Daddy.

"And look at that slippy slider! I was a slippy slider when I stayed on the sledge, wasn't I?"

"You were the *best* Slippy Slider!" laughed Daddy.

What a VERY BIG lake it was!
And what a lot of skaters!

They stopped at the edge of the lake and Daddy said. "Skates on, everyone!" But Bella was worried again.

Soon they were rushing down the hill with the wind whooshing in their ears. But suddenly they came to a bumpy bit.

Up in the air went Ben and Sophie.

And **down** they went – **plop** – into a snowdrift!

But Bella held on tight all the way to the bottom. *She* didn't fall off at all!

"Well done, my **Slippy Slider!**" laughed **Daddy**.

Then Ben and Sophie wanted to go sledging.
"Good idea!" said Daddy. "All aboard!"
And before Bella had time to start worrying,
off they went, sliding over the snow.

So Bella went outside with the others.
But instead of making a snow-rabbit . . .

. . . she made a snow-mouse!
That made everybody laugh.
"Well done, my Funny Bunny!"
said Daddy.

So Daddy said, "Don't worry, Little Baby Not-Sure.
Let's just have some fun in the snow first."
"Yes! Let's all make a snow-rabbit!" shouted
Ben and Sophie.

But Bella wouldn't put her hat and scarf on.

She still wasn't sure about skating.
What if she fell over and hurt herself?

Straight after breakfast Daddy said,
"Come on, little rabbits! Let's get ready
to go out."

"I'm the fastest!" said Ben.
"Well done, Big Brother
Rushabout!" said Daddy.

"And I look the smartest!" said Sophie.
"That's right, Big Sister Tidypaws!"
said Daddy.

But Bella just played with her porridge and she wouldn't eat her eggy soldiers. She still wasn't sure about skating. She only had little legs. What if she couldn't keep up?

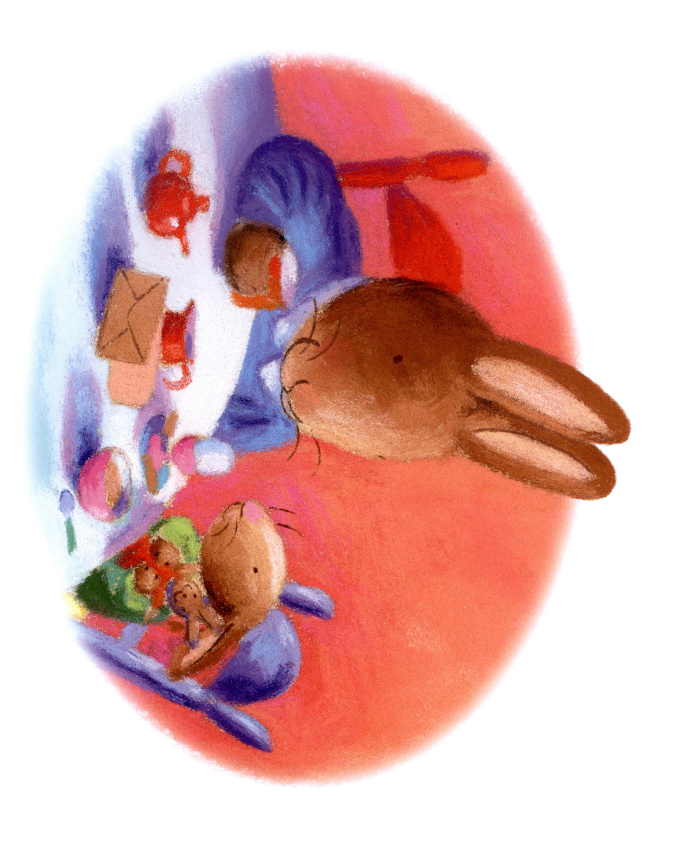

"I'm having *two* smoothies for breakfast," said Ben.

"I'm a speedy eater!"

"Well done, Big Brother Rushabout!" said Daddy.

Sophie ate up all her fruit and yoghurt without spilling one bit.

"Well done, Big Sister Tidypaws!" said Daddy.

But Bella was worried about skating.
What if she looked silly and everyone laughed at her?
"I'm not sure," she said.

"Don't worry, Little Baby Not-Sure," said Daddy.
"Eat a good breakfast and then you'll be ready
for skating."

One winter's morning Daddy said.
"Who wants to go ice skating today?
The lake is frozen hard!"

"Me me me!"
said Ben.

"Me me me!"
said Sophie.

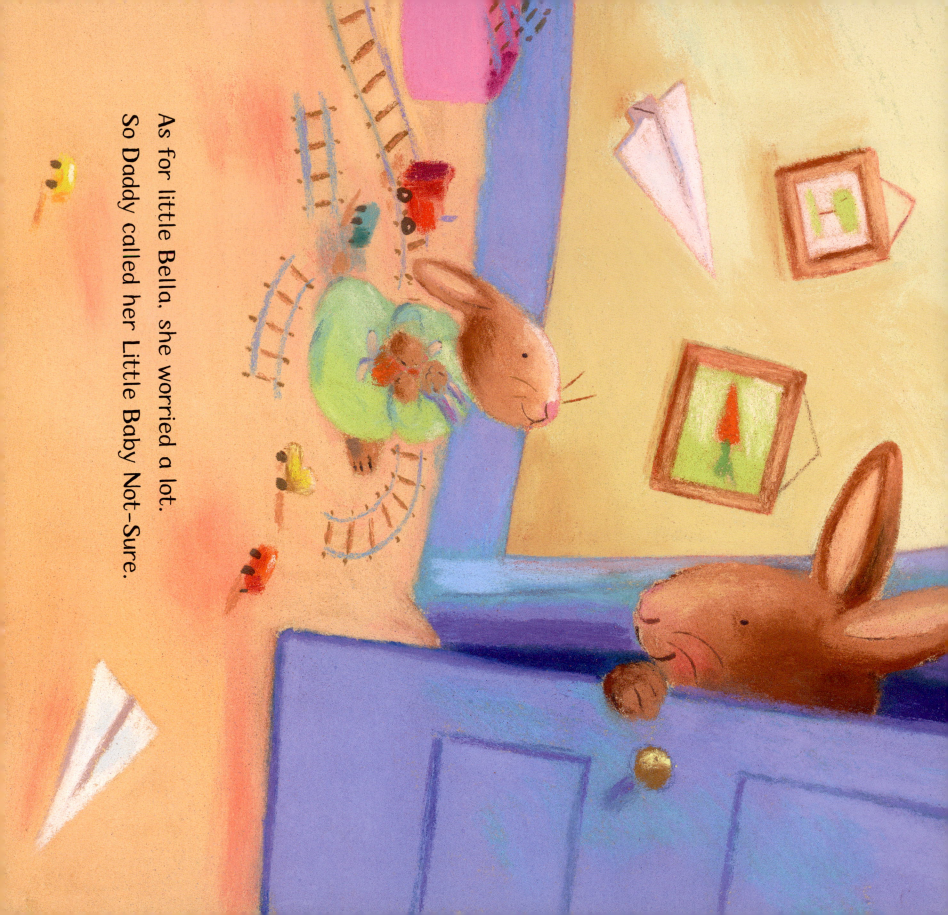

As for little Bella, she worried a lot.
So Daddy called her Little Baby Not-Sure.

Daddy Rabbit liked making up funny names for his little rabbits. Ben was always in a hurry, so Daddy called him Big Brother Rushabout.

Sophie was super neat, so Daddy called her Big Sister Tidypaws.

Ian Whybrow

Bella Gets Her Skates On

Illustrated by Rosie Reeve

MACMILLAN CHILDREN'S BOOKS

For Sophia and Amélie, with love – I.W.

To Peter and Mia, with love – R.R.

First published 2007 by Macmillan Children's Books
This edition published 2011 by Macmillan Children's Books
a division of Macmillan Publishers Limited
20 New Wharf Road, London N1 9RR
Basingstoke and Oxford
Associated companies throughout the world
www.panmacmillan.com

ISBN: 978-1-4472-8149-8

Text copyright © Ian Whybrow 2007
Illustrations copyright © Rosie Reeve 2007
Moral rights asserted.

3 5 7 9 8 6 4

A CIP catalogue record for this book
is available from the British Library.

Printed in China

Bella Gets Her Skates On

ST ANTON, AUSTRIA

The unicorns have a couple of free days in between tour stops, so they decide to try out their skills on the slopes at the picturesque resort of St Anton.

Leaf takes to the snow like a pro and heads off in search of something called a 'black run'. Amethyst is struggling to master the skis, even on the baby slopes, and after falling horn over hoof for the third time, she and Stardust trot off to get a head start on the après-ski activities.

Can you spot all of the unicorns?

VENICE, ITALY

Amethyst is delighted to be visiting Venice. Her favourite novel is set in this fairytale city and she's spent hours back in the Valley daydreaming of floating through the canals in a gondola. *So* romantic.

Some of the unicorns are spotted by a group of tourists in the Piazza San Marco, and Stardust is happy to greet the fans and sign autographs with his horn. Meanwhile, Ruby kicks back with a cappuccino and slice of tiramisu in the sun – bliss.

Can you spot all of the unicorns?

ALL ABOARD

The train has arrived to take the unicorns to their next exciting destination. Snowflake tells Blossom to watch their luggage while he trots off to collect the tickets, and Ruby goes in search of some tasty snacks for the journey.

Luna and Leaf amuse themselves by playing a game of hide-and-seek, and Luna is particuarly proud of the hiding spot she has chosen. Will Leaf find her in time to catch their train?

Can you spot all of the unicorns?

Café de Paris

PARIS, FRANCE

It doesn't take long for Luna to fall in love with Paris – the fashion, the food, the romance, the art. It couldn't be a more magical place.

While Blossom and Amethyst are planning which chic boutiques to visit first, Ruby is trying to persuade Stardust to climb the Eiffel Tower with her. He doesn't fancy the queues, and doesn't want to admit that he is scared of heights. He'd far rather while away the hours people watching from a cute café, with an ice-cold drink in hoof.

Can you spot all of the unicorns?

BOULANGERIE

DELPHI, GREECE

It's been a busy few days for the family in Greece, but they've found time to visit the Temple of Apollo. Some of the earliest recordings of unicorns were from ancient Greek writers, and it's a privilege for the blessing to have the opportunity to learn about their ancestors.

Hearing that the unicorns of Rainbow Valley were coming, the locals have staged a special performance in their honour, with impressive costumes and beautiful music. The unicorns can't wait to share some of their own wisdom and magic with the crowd.

Can you spot all of the unicorns?

GIZA, EGYPT

Ruby couldn't let a trip to Egypt pass without a visit to the mighty pyramids. She thinks the Great Sphinx of Giza, with the body of a lion and the head of a man, is the most magnificent statue she's ever seen.

Some of the other unicorns are less impressed. They're melting in the blistering heat and the humidity is giving Blossom's mane a mind of its own. Leaf is getting restless. He's bored of touring endless sights, but Snowflake has promised they'll do something more adventurous on their next stop.

Can you spot all of the unicorns?

WHITEWATER RAFTING

The blessing has signed up for a whitewater rafting adventure. Their guide promises it will be an unforgettable experience, but stresses that they must keep their horns away from the sides of the inflatable rafts. There is a high risk of causing a puncture.

Stardust anticipates it being an experience he'd rather forget. He hates being out of control, and those whirling rapids look SCARY! Meanwhile, daredevil Leaf is in his element – there's no stopping him as he paddles off at top speed down the thundering river.

Can you spot all of the unicorns?

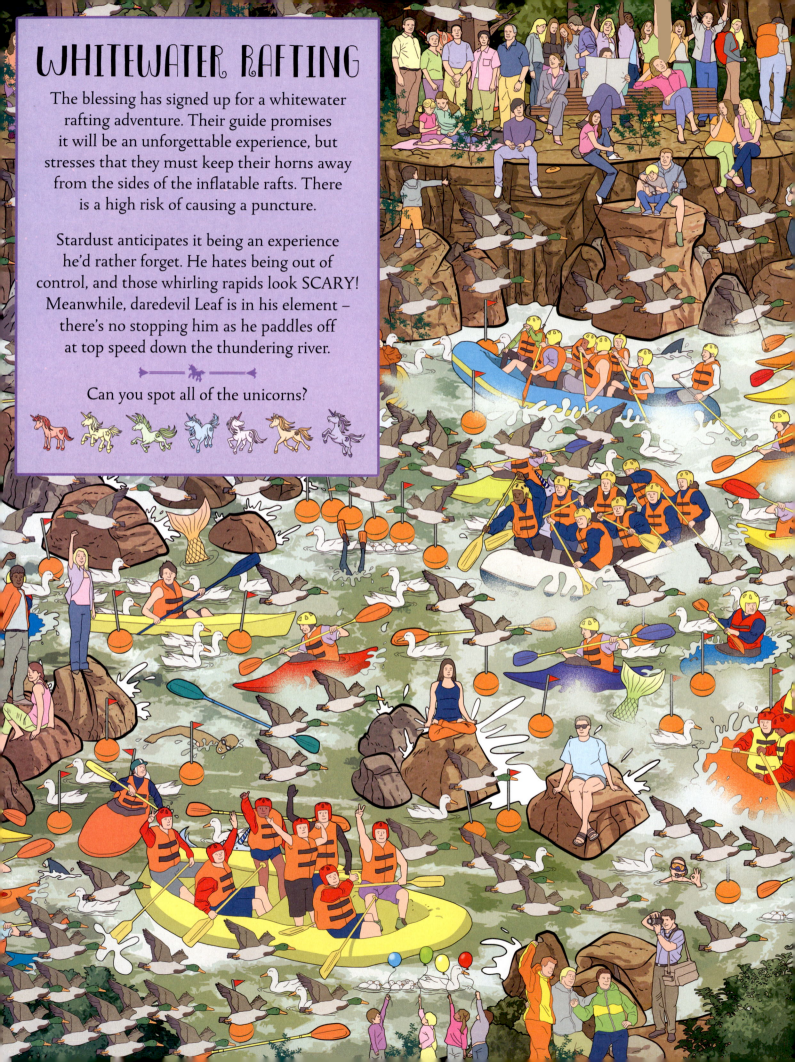

NEW YORK, USA

It's the end of a busy day for the unicorns in the Big Apple, with back-to-back press interviews and photoshoots. They even made a special appearance on a prime-time TV show.

Now it's time to let their manes down and hit the bright lights of Broadway. Luna loves the buzz of the city, with its cool neon signs and high-rise buildings. Leaf makes a beeline for Unicorner, a shop which claims to sell EVERYTHING unicorn related. He spots a poster advertising 'Unicorn World'. What could that be, he wonders?

Can you spot all of the unicorns?

SANTA CRUZ, USA

Stardust can see himself getting used to the laid-back, sunny Californian vibes. Everyone is so chilled out and friendly. He's already been offered a free surfing lesson while he was picking up a green juice at the beach café.

Ruby is ready to plunge horn-first into the sea, and Snowflake is busy trotting up and down the boardwalk, admiring the glorious vintage funfair. The sweet smell of candy floss reminds him of being back in Rainbow Valley.

Can you spot all of the unicorns?

RIO DE JANEIRO, BRAZIL

Carnival is in full swing when the blessing lands in Rio de Janeiro, and the unicorns are ready to PARTY! The streets are alive with people dancing, spectacular colours, jubilant music and incredible costumes. Amethyst has never seen so much glitter and sparkle – and that's unusual for a unicorn.

Leaf and Stardust are trying to master samba dancing, but they keep tripping over their hooves. Everyone makes it look so easy, but moving their hips and legs to the rhythm of the drums is not coming naturally to the unicorns.

Can you spot all of the unicorns?

A FILM SET SURPRISE

The blessing has just been interviewed for a documentary on the Magical Channel, but after the unicorns leave the studio, they find themselves in a bizarre situation. As they trot past a film set for a period drama, the director comes running after them. Some of the stunt horses for the next scene are stuck in a traffic jam and the crew need replacements urgently.

The unicorns are whisked through mane and make-up and told to blend in with the crowd. Before they know it the cameras are rolling. LIGHTS, CAMERA, ACTION!

Can you spot all of the unicorns?

UNDER THE SEA

After much persuasion from Leaf, all seven unicorns have taken the plunge and gone diving on the Great Barrier Reef in Australia. Luna is especially anxious, but Leaf reassures her that her horn will act as a snorkle.

Ruby is enjoying the tranquility and silence of being under the sea – it's like another world. Amethyst is transfixed by the rainbow-coloured fish and beautiful coral, while Stardust is trying to track down something called a narwhal – the unicorn of the sea, apparently.

Can you spot all of the unicorns?

DINOSAUR FUN

It's the blessing's last day in Australia and Ruby has organized a trip to a dinosaur museum. The exhibit promises to transport visitors back to the prehistoric world, but the whole experience is a bit too realistic for poor Blossom. The unicorns are surrounded by giant, moving dinosaurs and she's terrified!

Luna isn't phased by the mighty beasts and Stardust has got horn envy. Did the *Triceratops* really need three horns? It's rather showy, in his opinion.

Can you spot all of the unicorns?

UNICORN WORLD

The family are coming to the end of their trip, but there's a final surprise in store. They've been invited to officially open 'Unicorn World', a magical place dedicated to the unicorns of Rainbow Valley, created by the Horse Collective – the unicorns' ultimate super-fan club.

The blessing is overwhelmed by the number of horses who've turned out to welcome them. It's a special moment as the sun begins to set behind the glistening rainbow. The tour has been an incredible experience and the memories will stay with the unicorns forever.

Can you spot all of the unicorns?

ANSWERS

SPOTTER'S CHECKLIST

- A monkey-shaped package ☐
- A man with a mop ☐
- A woman holding pink flowers ☐
- A man proposing to his girlfriend ☐
- Two plane spotters ☐
- A child wearing a red cap ☐
- A girl with a big teddy bear ☐
- Three 'no entry' signs ☐
- Two purple suitcases ☐
- A woman eating an apple ☐

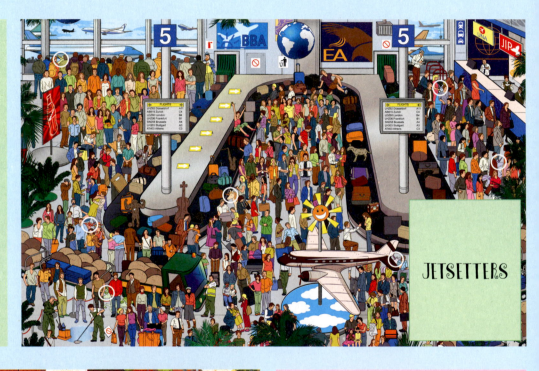

JETSETTERS

VIP TREATMENT

SPOTTER'S CHECKLIST

- Someone building a house of cards ☐
- A man on a tiny bike ☐
- A man with a guitar case ☐
- A child drawing on hotel property ☐
- A woman doing the vacuuming ☐
- Someone yelling at the hotel manager ☐
- Someone riding on a hotel trolley ☐
- A waiter with a bottle of champagne ☐
- A man playing the violin ☐
- A child standing on a chair ☐

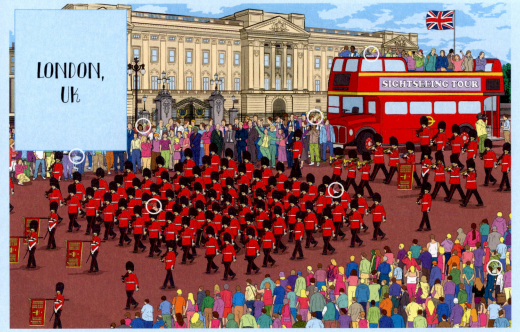

SPOTTER'S CHECKLIST

- A news reporter ☐
- A blue trumpet ☐
- A lost camera ☐
- A guard in the wrong trousers ☐
- A man hugging his daughter ☐
- A girl sucking her thumb ☐
- Two Union Jack flags ☐
- A sunburnt man ☐
- Some stripy trousers ☐
- A purple rucksack ☐

SPOTTER'S CHECKLIST

- Cups of coffee being spilt ☐
- A man eating a bag of doughnuts ☐
- Two alpine rescue doctors ☐
- A red and yellow snowboard ☐
- A man with a red bow tie ☐
- Someone relaxing on the ski lift ☐
- Some dangerous driving ☐
- A child learning to ski ☐
- A snowboarder with a goatee beard ☐
- A man getting his hat knocked off ☐

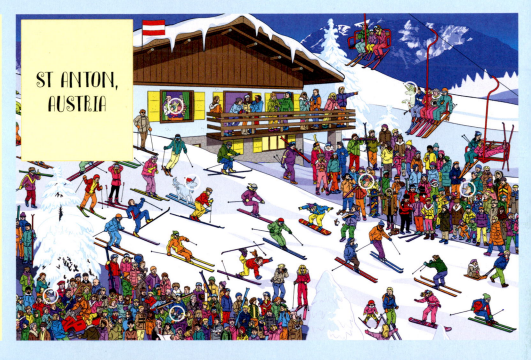

ST ANTON, AUSTRIA

VENICE, ITALY

SPOTTER'S CHECKLIST

- A monk ☐
- A man with mismatched shoes ☐
- A polka-dot costume ☐
- A violinist ☐
- A polka-dot tie ☐
- One yellow glove ☐
- Four couples holding hands ☐
- Two gold masks ☐
- A girl in purple waiting for her date ☐
- A waitress on her way home ☐

SPOTTER'S CHECKLIST

ALL ABOARD

- A man falling over on the stairs ☐
- A woman carrying a stack of presents ☐
- A couple arguing ☐
- A girl with pink hair ☐
- A boy playing with a toy train ☐
- Two people eating ice cream ☐
- A man on a bike ☐
- A guard with a flag ☐
- Two people sliding down the banisters ☐
- Someone carrying a skateboard ☐

SPOTTER'S CHECKLIST

- A birthday cake ☐
- A cat among the pigeons ☐
- A man with a walking stick ☐
- A man on a laptop ☐
- A saxophone player ☐
- A woman eating crisps ☐
- A man with a purple briefcase ☐
- Lost boys with a map ☐
- A woman with pink sunglasses ☐
- A man sweeping ☐

PARIS, FRANCE

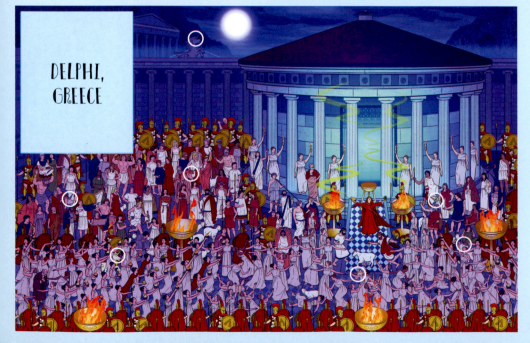

DELPHI, GREECE

SPOTTER'S CHECKLIST

- The Pythia, the priestess of the oracle ☐
- Two people meditating ☐
- A man with wings on his helmet ☐
- A woman on a man's shoulders ☐
- A woman reading a scroll ☐
- A man with a trident ☐
- A man waving ☐
- Thirteen goats ☐
- A man tripping up ☐
- A soldier whose helmet is on fire ☐

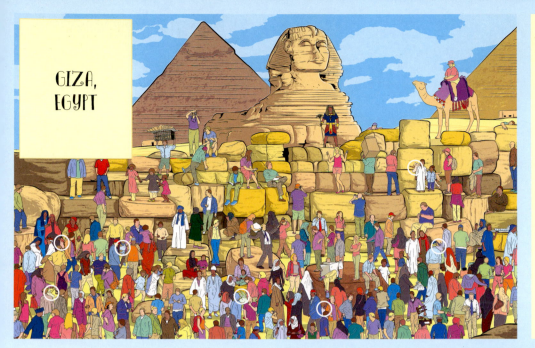

GIZA, EGYPT

SPOTTER'S CHECKLIST

A boy with a finger trap ☐

A modern-day pharaoh ☐

A man toppling over backwards ☐

A boy with a tray of basbousa cakes ☐

A man on his mobile phone ☐

A girl scratching her head ☐

A man with a large cardboard box ☐

A tiny mummy ☐

A child on her mother's shoulders ☐

A man in an orange cowboy hat ☐

SPOTTER'S CHECKLIST

A woman meditating ☐

Three mermaids ☐

A baseball glove ☐

A man snorkelling ☐

A man holding a football ☐

A horse ☐

Two men abseiling ☐

Someone reading the newspaper ☐

A purple kite ☐

Four balloons ☐

WHITEWATER RAFTING

NEW YORK, USA

SPOTTER'S CHECKLIST

Four taxis ☐

A clock ☐

A woman jogging ☐

A boy reading a map ☐

A man taking a photo ☐

A brown baseball cap ☐

A red sports car ☐

A police officer ☐

Some dropped litter ☐

A girl in a bobble hat ☐

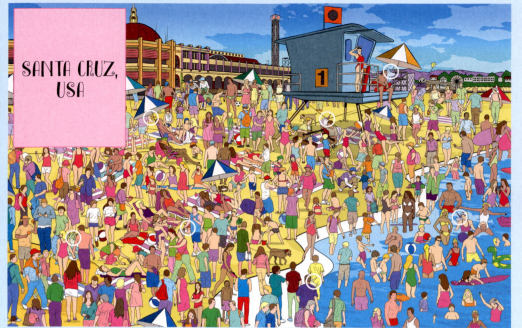

SANTA CRUZ, USA

SPOTTER'S CHECKLIST

- A yellow kite ☐
- A bodybuilder ☐
- A human pyramid ☐
- A stray dog ☐
- A man with a frisbee ☐
- A boy with turtle armbands ☐
- A football ☐
- Someone who can't swim ☐
- A guitar-jamming session ☐
- A man carrying green shoes ☐

SPOTTER'S CHECKLIST

- A man in a green wig ☐
- Sixteen blue balloons ☐
- A woman with a purple handbag ☐
- A drummer ☐
- An orange baseball cap ☐
- Some tasselled trousers ☐
- A polka-dot bikini ☐
- White elbow gloves ☐
- An orange bag ☐
- A dancer with mismatched shoes ☐

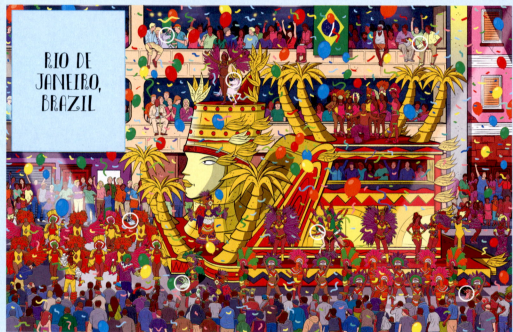

RIO DE JANEIRO, BRAZIL

A FILM SET SURPRISE

SPOTTER'S CHECKLIST

- Someone playing a harp ☐
- Some sandwiches ☐
- A woman with lilac hair ☐
- A man with a loudspeaker ☐
- Someone wearing a red scarf ☐
- A musketeer on the phone ☐
- Someone holding a basket ☐
- Two actors having make-up done ☐
- A man falling down the stairs ☐
- A teapot ☐

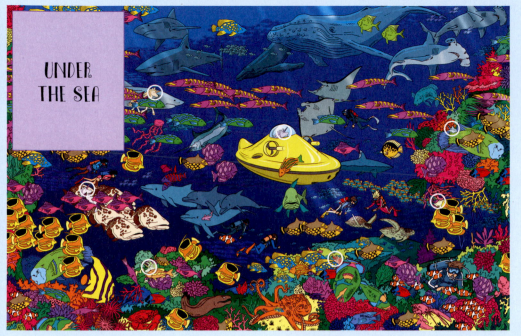

UNDER THE SEA

SPOTTER'S CHECKLIST

A pink lobster ☐

Two fish with big pink lips ☐

An ugly eel ☐

A jellyfish ☐

A swordfish ☐

A dawdling clownfish ☐

A red crab ☐

Seven fish with a diamond pattern ☐

Two turtles ☐

A pair of yellow flippers ☐

SPOTTER'S CHECKLIST

A dino with a bright mohican ☐

A dino relaxing on its back ☐

Five dragonflies ☐

A tiny dino climbing high ☐

A dino trampling on another's head ☐

Three flying dinosaurs ☐

A *Stegosaurus* ☐

A *Triceratops* ☐

An *Allosaurus* ☐

Four green dinos wading in the water ☐

DINOSAUR FUN

UNICORN WORLD

SPOTTER'S CHECKLIST

A superhero horse ☐

A human shoe ☐

Two snorkelling horses ☐

Three pink satchels ☐

A wizard horse ☐

A kite ☐

Two golden horseshoes ☐

A unicorn onesie ☐

A foal being carried ☐

A ballerina horse ☐

Published in Great Britain in 2018 by Michael O'Mara Books Limited,
9 Lion Yard, Tremadoc Road, London SW4 7NQ

W www.mombooks.com
f Michael O'Mara Books
@OMaraBooks

Additional artwork by Stuart Taylor, Wan (Big Red Illustration) and Steve Wiltshire

A CIP catalogue record for this book is available from the British Library.

ISBN: 978-1-78243-995-0

3 5 7 9 10 8 6 4 2

This book was printed in August 2018 by Shenzhen Wing King
Tong Paper Products Co. Ltd., Shenzhen, Guangdong, China.